P9-EJT-471

Best Places to Bird
in the Prairies

CALGARY PUBLIC LIBRARY

MAY - - 2018

Local experts
Insider knowledge
Hard-to-find birds

John Acorn, Alan Smith
& Nicola Koper

BEST PLACES TO BIRD IN THE PRAIRIES

Foreword by CANDACE SAVAGE

GREYSTONE BOOKS

Vancouver/Berkeley

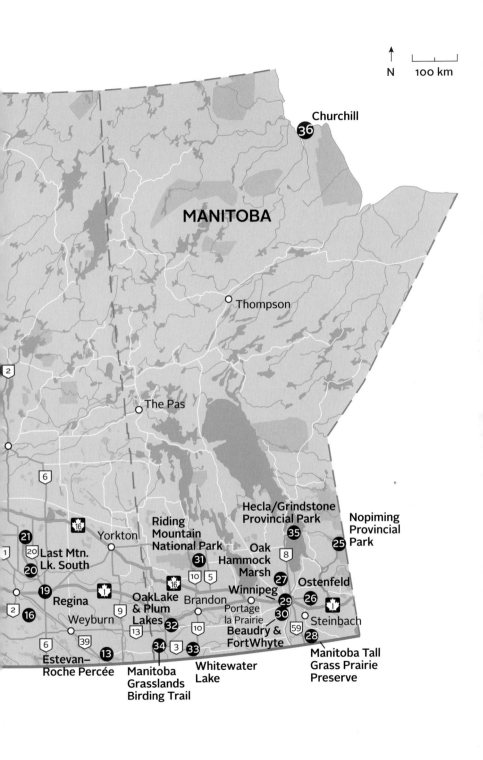

N   100 km

Churchill **36**

MANITOBA

Thompson

2

The Pas

6

Hecla/Grindstone
Provincial Park

35

Nopiming
Provincial
Park

25

Riding
Mountain
National Park

Oak
Hammock
Marsh

8

Ostenfeld

27

21

16

Yorkton

31

10 5

26

20

Last Mtn.
Lk. South

16

Winnipeg

29

1

20

OakLake
& Plum
Lakes

Brandon

Portage
la Prairie

30

Steinbach

19

9

32

10

28

2 **16**

Regina

Beaudry &
FortWhyte

59

Weyburn

13

34 3 **33**

6

39

Estevan–
Roche Percée

13

Manitoba
Grasslands
Birding Trail

Whitewater
Lake

Manitoba Tall
Grass Prairie
Preserve

FOREWORD

Y OU HEARD IT here first: Canada's three midwestern provinces are a paradise for birdwatchers. We're talking about a region that spans 1.8 million square km (almost 700,000 square mi.), more than three times the size of France, and an immense territory that invites superlatives. To the north, broad swaths of boreal and mixed-wood forests receive an annual influx of migrating songbirds, millions upon millions of them, drawn to some of the richest and most productive breeding grounds anywhere in the world. Farther south, wide-open expanses of prairie provide living space for grassland specialists like Greater Sage-Grouse and Long-billed Curlews, permitting them to extend their range into northerly latitudes. Meanwhile, the region's thousands

◀ Rock Wrens do indeed prefer rocky places, such as canyons and badlands.
GERALD ROMANCHUK

of prairie potholes, or wetlands, are home to enormous flocks of ducks that hatch out most of the ducklings on the continent. Add in rugged mountains, active sand dunes, even a strip of Arctic coast, and it becomes easy to understand why birdwatching in the so-called "Prairie provinces" can provide a lifetime of fascination and happiness.

And yet, it would be easy to miss out on all the fun if you didn't know where to look. As impressively varied as the region is, it's also a country of broad strokes, long distances, and deceptive sameness, and it can pass us by in a blur, an endless dull streak on the far side of the car window. That's why the book that you have in your hands is so welcome and valuable. In these pages, three seasoned birders, each an expert on his or her own home province, offer detailed introductions to their own personal birding hot spots. Some of their recommendations are almost mandatory—an array of national, provincial, and municipal parks, for example, or Manitoba's famous Oak Hammock Marsh—but others are wonderfully quirky. Who wouldn't want to hang out in a decaying industrial site with John Acorn, watching Gyrfalcons and Prairie Falcons strike at pigeons (mostly without success) or to head down an ever-dwindling trail with Alan Smith to look for Belted Kingfishers at the confluence of the South Saskatchewan and Red Deer Rivers? Who wouldn't want to help Nicola Koper check Assiniboine School in Winnipeg for nesting Chimney Swifts? It's exciting to be trusted with this kind of insider information.

I've spent most of my life in the Prairie provinces, and though I'm not a Very Serious Birder—no life list or target species for me—I usually have my binoculars and bird book within easy reach. I know a marsh from a meadow, a cowbird from a chickadee. And yet, thanks to the generosity of these authors, I am reminded how much I have yet to discover and how thrilling those discoveries can be. For instance, it says right here that Harlequin Ducks, which I've never seen and which are spectacular, have sometimes been spotted on the river not far from my home. So now, if you'll excuse me, I'll look forward to seeing you later, out on the birding trail.

CANDACE SAVAGE
Saskatoon, Saskatchewan
July 2017

INTRODUCTION

A JOURNEY THROUGH
THE PRAIRIE PROVINCES

MANY CANADIANS WHO haven't travelled through Alberta, Saskatchewan, and Manitoba think of the Prairies as a monotonous monoculture of wheat, but the three Prairie provinces actually form a vast and diverse landscape. Travelling across the Prairie provinces offers an always-changing birdscape. There are broad, largely unseen boundaries between eastern and western species, the legacy of the recolonization of northern North America after the retreat of the Pleistocene ice sheets. The journey north takes you from hot desert grasslands through a wide variety of forests to the harsh tundras of the Arctic. And with a diversity in landforms from flat plains to some of the most spectacular mountains in the world comes a

◄ Snowy egrets are a rare but welcome visitor to our Prairie provinces.
ILYA POVALYAEV

I

multitude of habitats that support some of the most diverse breeding bird faunas in North America.

Southeastern Manitoba marks the western extent of eastern hardwood forests, home to species such as Eastern Screech-Owl, Wood Thrush, and Scarlet Tanager. The moister grasslands of southern Manitoba, with species such as Bobolink, give way as you move west to the drier grasslands of southern Saskatchewan and southern Alberta, where Sprague's Pipits and Chestnut-collared Longspurs sing above the plains. And in southwestern Saskatchewan and southeastern Alberta, the dry, shortgrass prairies are home to species such as McCown's Longspurs and Brewer's Sparrows.

The boreal forest extends in a broad arc from central Manitoba west to northern Alberta. These forests are highly diverse on even a local scale, with a rich mixture of pine, spruce, birch, and aspen forests, thousands of lakes, marshes, and other wetlands, and a mosaic of grasslands along their southern border. Many species of warblers occupy different forest types, while Great Gray Owls hunt in forest openings and Yellow Rails call from wet sedge meadows.

Along the Hudson Bay coast of northern Manitoba is a strip of Arctic tundra that offers exciting birding possibilities for southern birders. Tundra Swans, Snow Geese, and Common Eiders nest along the coast, while Smith's Longspurs and American Tree Sparrows sing from the shrubby tundra.

And at the western edge of Alberta is another landform that many don't associate with the Prairie provinces—the towering wall of the Rocky Mountains. The mountain forests differ from the boreal forests in their strongly western fauna, with birds such as Dusky Grouse, Red-naped Sapsuckers, and Townsend's Warblers. As you climb higher, the alpine tundra hosts Horned Larks and American Pipits as the Arctic tundra does, but the White-tailed Ptarmigan is found only in these treeless islands atop high peaks.

Therefore calling Alberta, Saskatchewan, and Manitoba the "Prairie provinces" is quite misleading, as there is so much diversity to explore and discover for novice and expert birders alike. Each chapter in this book represents a small piece of this brilliant avian mosaic, told from the perspective of local birders willing to share their local secrets with you—the reader.

May your travels through the heart of Canada be delightful, safe, and filled with birds!

—RICHARD CANNINGS *and* RUSSELL CANNINGS

eBIRD

The growing popularity of "eBird" (a worldwide public database for recording bird sightings) has given birders yet another resource with which to access the latest bird sightings and trends from any given area. Create an account for free at eBird.ca, and then explore the user-friendly site to find out where your target birds have been seen most recently.

BIRDING ETHICS

Anyone who gets enjoyment from birds cares about them in some way, so naturally all of us should take steps to ensure that our activities have a minimal impact on the habitats we visit. The American Birding Association has a "Code of Birding Ethics" that are quite suitable for birding pursuits around the world. Much of it involves common sense (e.g., "Respect the law")—however, we think it important to emphasize the following:

1(b) To avoid stressing birds or exposing them to danger, exercise restraint and caution during observation, photography, sound recording, or filming.

Limit the use of recordings and other methods of attracting birds, and never use such methods in heavily birded areas, or for attracting any species that is Threatened, Endangered, or of Special Concern, or is rare in your local area.

Keep well back from nests and nesting colonies, roosts, display areas, and important feeding sites. In such sensitive areas, if there is a need for extended observation, photography, filming, or recording, try to use a blind or hide, and take advantage of natural cover.

Use artificial light sparingly for filming or photography, especially for close-ups.

A pair of Turkey Vultures display at their nest site near Last Mountain Lake.
ALAN R. SMITH

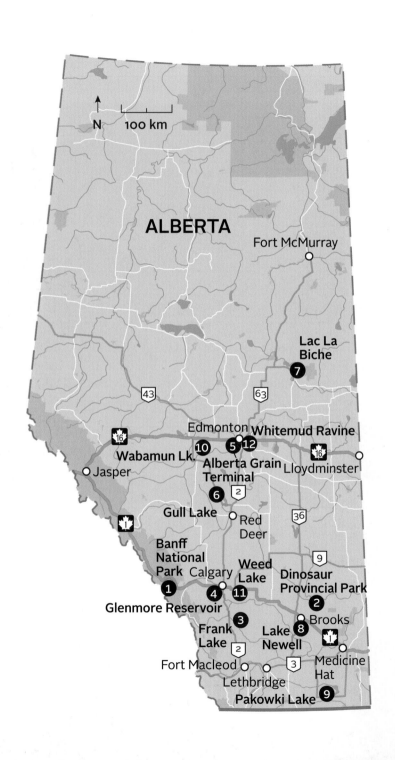

N   100 km

ALBERTA

Fort McMurray

Lac La
Biche
7

43   63

Edmonton Whitemud Ravine
16
10 **5** **12**
Wabamun Lk.   16
Alberta Grain   Lloydminster
Jasper   Terminal

6   2
Gull Lake   36
Red
Deer
9
Banff
National   Weed
Park Calgary   Lake   Dinosaur
Provincial Park
1 **4** **11**
Glenmore Reservoir   **2**
Brooks
3 **8**
Frank   Lake
Lake   Newell   **1**
2
Fort Macleod   3   Medicine
Hat
Lethbridge
Pakowki Lake   **9**

ALBERTA

JOHN ACORN

—1—
BANFF NATIONAL PARK

W HEN IT COMES to birding in Alberta, it's hard not to think of the Rocky Mountains. After all, most visitors to Alberta head straight to Banff or Jasper for the scenery. You can find all of the signature bird species of the Rockies in any of the mountain parks (Banff, Jasper, Waterton, and Kananaskis Country), but my favourite Rocky Mountain destination is still Banff.

Mountain naturalists think in terms of three altitudinal zones. The lowest is the montane, where the town of Banff lies, along with most of the park's roads and hotels. This is

◄ Gray-crowned Rosy-Finches move up- and downslope with the seasons and the weather. GERALD ROMANCHUK

mountains-in-the-background birding, and the birds here are abundant and delightful. On one visit to the Cave and Basin Trail this past summer, my student Sydney Mohr and I had close-up views of Mountain Chickadees, Townsend's Warblers, and Ruby-crowned Kinglets, and then, much to our delight, we spotted nine Soras, including babies, from the blind down at the marsh. In winter, my birding buddy Brian Leishman and I have seen everything from Rusty Blackbirds to Virginia Rails here, all attracted by the year-round flow of water. Harlequin Ducks and American Dippers need larger streams and rivers, and they sometimes pop up along the Bow River, or faster streams upslope. Spend enough time in the Banff area and you'll spot them, as well as Calliope Hummingbirds, which seem to like shrubby areas near water.

The mid-altitude zone is called the subalpine, and to me it's the least exciting, covered largely by continuous forests of Lodgepole Pine, and of only moderate interest to birds and birders. However, there are wonderful lakes in this zone, including the famous Lake Louise, and the almost-as-famous Lake Minnewanka. Here, you'll have a chance of seeing some of the true mountain species, such as Clark's Nutcracker, Steller's Jay, and Gray-crowned Rosy-Finch, as well as plenty of Osprey and Common Loons around the lakes.

For the high-altitude species, you need to get up to treeline and above, in the alpine zone. Here, you might find a White-tailed Ptarmigan, or a Timberline Sparrow. If you have time, do visit Jasper, Waterton, and Kananaskis as well—you never know what you might spot.

BIRDING GUIDE

After entering the park, admiring the scenery along the highway, watching for roadside birds such as Bald Eagles and Gray Jays, and making your way to the town, begin with the Cave and Basin Trail. Make sure you're on the pedestrian trail and not the horse trail. The interpretive exhibits in the visitor centre are worth seeing, although the emphasis here is on human history rather than natural history. The trail itself isn't very long, and most of it consists of a well-maintained boardwalk. Make your way down to the blind overlooking the marsh, and spend enough time there to allow nearby birds to come out of hiding. The longer you linger, the more you'll see. In spring and summer, be alert for warblers and sparrows along the trail. In winter, watch for such remarkable species as Virginia Rail along the creek. I remember one right beside the trail, apparently unfazed by the presence of people.

On the other side of town, take the short (about 3 km/1.8 mi.) drive along the Vermilion Lakes, stopping from time to time to scan both the water and the trees. In winter, watch for spring-fed open patches—they may have interesting birds around them. There are numerous small lakes in the park, but you should also visit Lake Minnewanka and Lake Louise, preferably outside of midsummer when it gets very crowded in the park. The trails around the lakes are especially nice, even in busier periods, as most tourists don't have the energy to move far from the parking lot.

The Bow River runs through the park, and is most easily accessible at the Bow Falls and in the townsite. Various other trails throughout the park will get you to other streams, and although it's often crowded, I recommend the trail at Johnston Canyon. In past years, a Black Swift nest was visible at eye level, in the cliff face across the stream, and there may be more nests to discover by now.

Bow Lake, at treeline, is worth a look, and all the birding action is remarkably close to the parking lot. In winter, the short willows near the lake are often home to White-tailed Ptarmigan, and if your experience is typical, it will be easier to spot them from their tracks than to see them against the white of the snow. This is also a good place to see Clark's Nutcrackers, and in summer, Fox Sparrows.

GETTING THERE

Banff lies about 130 km (80 mi.) west of Calgary, on Hwy. 1, the Trans-Canada Hwy. Two exits lead to Banff townsite. If you turn north/right instead of left, the first will also take you to Lake Minnewanka, via RR (Range Road) 115B and the Lake Minnewanka Scenic Dr., which is a loop road.

If you take the westernmost of the two exits off the highway to Banff townsite, you find yourself on Mount Norquay Rd., which becomes Lynx St., and then Bear St. as it enters the town (hey, it's a federal government park—why should it make sense?). Take Bear St. to Buffalo St., turn left, and then right on Banff Ave. Cross the Bow River over the bridge, and then turn right on Cave Ave. (which has another name, Spray Ave., if you turn left) to get to the Cave and Basin parking lot.

To get to the Vermilion Lakes, retrace your path to Mount Norquay Rd. and take Vermilion Lakes Rd. southwest from there. It runs alongside the lakes for about 3 km (1.8 mi.), and dead-ends in a turnaround.

Lake Louise is about a 40-minute drive farther west on the Trans-Canada Hwy., and Bow Lake is another 50 km (31 mi.) or so up Hwy. 93 from Lake Louise townsite.

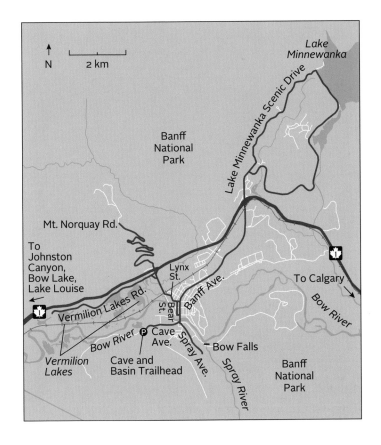

Yellow-breasted Chats are loud, with big personalities. GERALD ROMANCHUK

2

DINOSAUR PROVINCIAL PARK

ES, IT'S TRUE: birds were the only group of dinosaurs to survive the mass extinction 66 million years ago. Dinosaurs are defined as all descendants of the first dinosaur, which lived more than 230 million years ago. Since the ancestors of birds were small theropods (bipedal meat-eating dinosaurs), birds are technically dinosaurs, as odd as that may seem. Many of the finest dinosaur fossils on earth have come from the badlands at Dinosaur Provincial Park, which is why the park was made a UNESCO World Heritage Site in 1979. But fossils were not the only reason for its designation; riparian cottonwood forests and their songbird populations were also mentioned in the original designation, as were the extensive badlands themselves and their resident birds of prey (Golden Eagle, Ferruginous Hawk, and Prairie Falcon, for example).

Until they reach the viewpoint, most visitors have no idea what they're about to see here. The flat grasslands north of Patricia suddenly give way to a truly magnificent vista of bare, beautifully layered badland hills, stretching away almost to the horizon. This is the biggest area of badlands in Canada, and the birds here are wonderful. They include not only diurnal raptors, but also Common Nighthawk, Great Horned Owl, Say's Phoebe, Rock Wren, and Lark Sparrow. If you're lucky, you might see a pair of Mountain Bluebirds nesting in a erosion hole in a sandstone hillside. On one of our fall trips, three in our party (but not me, dang it!) spotted a White-throated Swift over the badlands. At the time of that sighting, a member of this species had only recently been seen in Alberta for the first time ever.

The badlands are the main draw here, but the riverine riparian forests are also spectacular. Plains Cottonwood forests provide a tremendous environment for songbirds, with shrubbier stands of willows, thorny buffaloberry, and Manitoba Maple here and there, in which you might spot a Yellow-breasted Chat. In places, the area between the forests and the badlands takes the form of sage flats, extensive muddy plains dotted with sagebrush and loaded with birds, including Ring-necked Pheasants.

Of course, the river itself is worth checking for birds, including Great Blue Heron, American White Pelican, Common Merganser, and Wood Duck. I first visited the park in 1975, and I still get excited every time I return.

BIRDING GUIDE

Birding at Dinosaur begins at prairie level, and I like to stop at the main viewpoint to scan for eagles and falcons, and to listen for Sprague's Pipit. Often, you'll see Loggerhead Shrike on your way to or from the park.

The best places to bird the badlands include the Badlands Trail itself and the valley of the Little Sandhill Creek. You're also welcome to prowl around the badlands within the central core area of the park, and many people enjoy scrambling around on the hills. Watch your step, though, and stay out of the badlands when they're wet—the bentonite clay swells with moisture and becomes extremely slippery. A guided tour into the natural preserve is worth your time, and the small fee, but it won't necessarily lead you to bird species you haven't already seen in the core.

The riverine forests are most accessible by walking along the Cottonwood Flats Trail, but they also extend into the campground, albeit without much understory. Making your way through these forests without a trail is difficult, and you might be surprised how many rattlesnakes prefer this environment to the badlands proper.

A wonderful patch of cottonwood forest surrounds the minimally developed campsite at the west end of the park, referred to as Steveville. Birding there is always good, and although there is no public access to the badlands here, you can scan for raptors and Violet-green Swallows from where TWP Rd. 220A comes close to the edge of the badlands.

Dinosaur Park is spectacular during the breeding season, but worth visiting at any time of year. I make an annual winter day trip, and over the years I've had great encounters with Sharp-tailed Grouse, Golden Eagle, Northern Goshawk, Prairie Falcon, Gyrfalcon, and Northern Shrike, especially around Steveville.

GETTING THERE

The closest large town is Brooks, along the Trans-Canada Hwy., 43 km (almost 27 mi.) away. From Brooks, head north on Hwy. 873, then east on Hwy. 544 to Patricia. To reach the park, turn north off Hwy. 544 on RR 130 just east of Patricia, and follow the park signs north and east. The access road passes the entrance viewpoint and descends into the badlands to the visitor centre, and the combined shower and concession building, day use area, and campground. A loop road runs through most of the core area, with the Badlands Trail to the south of the loop and the Cottonwood Flats trail to the north. Much of the park is in the natural preserve, which is off-limits without a guided tour (arranged through the visitor centre). The foot trail up the valley of the Little Sandhill Creek starts at the far end of the group camping area and is currently marked by a No Bicycles sign.

To reach the western, or Steveville, end of the park, head back to the west side of Patricia on Hwy. 544, then north on Hwy. 876, following along until you cross the Red Deer River. The campground is in the cottonwoods to the northeast of the bridge, and past the campground you can take TWP Rd. 220A to the east, at least for a kilometre or two, although the grassland birding is pretty good farther on as well.

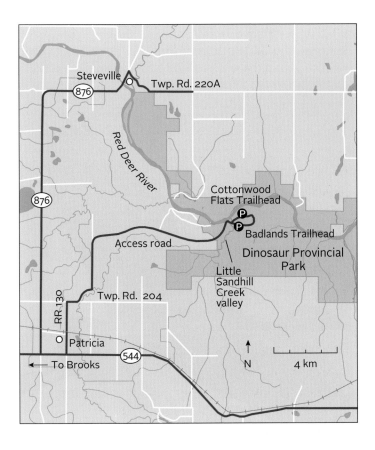

The iridescence on a flying White-faced Ibis can be striking. JOHN ACORN

3

FRANK LAKE

N OT FAR FROM Calgary, Frank Lake is another classic Alberta birding destination, and this book would not be complete without it. Well, actually, this book is far from complete, because it's just a select offering of top spots, but it wouldn't be complete *enough* without it. Frank Lake itself is the result of a waterfowl and wetland conservation project, undertaken by Ducks Unlimited, with the help of numerous other partner organizations, back in the 1980s. In other words, it's an artificial reservoir, not a natural lake. This probably explains the utterly uninspired names for the three lake basins: Basin 1, Basin 2, and Basin 3. Everything here has been optimized for the breeding success of game birds, but the spinoff benefits for other wetland birds, not to mention non-avian plants and animals, are impressive. Of course, birders, and especially bird photographers, also benefit. On a busy day in springtime, with all the birds in their breeding plumages, the observation blind can be a very popular place indeed.

On a recent visit to Frank Lake, I joined my birding friends Brian Leishman and Chris Fisher. We had brought fresh coffee from nearby High River, and we settled in for a nice, long session. For most of the visit we had the blind to ourselves, and we got great looks at a variety of ducks (I was especially pleased with the close-up views of Ruddy Ducks and Northern Shovelers) as well as White-faced Ibis, Black-necked Stilts, and Eared Grebes. Even the American Coots were putting on a great show, gathering food for their babies. In early June, baby coots have bald orange heads and stringy orange beards, and they're so darned ugly that they're adorable. Only baby Soras come close.

While we were admiring and photographing the birds, a pleasant couple from the UK stopped by, having heard how great this place can be. We helped them identify a few things, and they went away happy.

For some reason, though, the blind is on the north end of the lake, facing south. Photographers would much rather place the sun behind them. That being said, on a day with diffuse high clouds, the lighting can be lovely from any direction, and I did get some nice photos of the iridescence of flying ibis when I was there with Brian and Chris.

BIRDING GUIDE

The observation blind is clearly the main draw, so you might as well begin here and plan to spend more than just a few minutes. If you're alone, it may take the birds a while to become accustomed to your presence. If the place is crowded, it may take time to get into an optimum position. There's also a trail that leads to the water's edge. It branches off from the main access road where the road widens enough to park a vehicle or two. The area here is open and marshy, but if you can manage not to spook the birds, you might get some good views from the walking trail, not to mention the benefits of being in the open yourself. This is a good area for American Avocets. There are two more access points, one on Basin 1 and one on Basin 3. If you're the sort of person who wants to "work" the area, you'll want to visit these as well.

GETTING THERE

The viewpoint and blind, on Basin 1, are easy to find—take Hwy. 23 about 6 km (3.5 mi.) straight east of High River, and turn off onto the gravel road that looks like a service road (530 Ave. East, also known as TWP Rd. 190), just before the highway curves toward the north. After the gate (which is locked at certain times of year but always open for foot access) there's a long gravel road flanked by boulders. This is the main access road. Partway along there's a wider area where you can park and foot trails that lead down to the water's edge, to the south. At the end of the road is a loop, where you'll find two porta-potties, a picnic table, and room to park. The observation blind is a very short distance from the parking area. You can also access Basin 1 by returning to Hwy. 23 and proceeding east and then turning south on what was probably once RR 274 (note that it doesn't appear

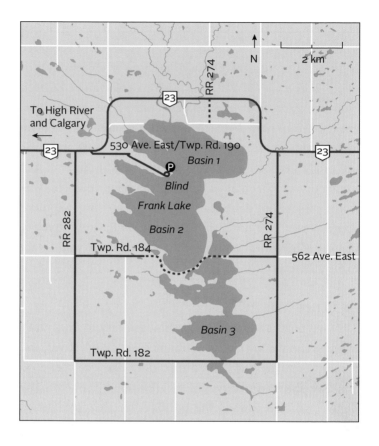

on Google Maps but it's obvious when you're driving). Access to the south end of Basin 3 involves getting onto 562 Ave. East, also known as TWP Rd. 184. To reach this road, turn south off of Hwy. 23 on RR 282 or RR 274. Things are actually a lot simpler once you're there, but don't expect these roads to look much like they do on the entrance sign map at the gate.

A baby coot, with orange beard and bald head, so ugly it is beautiful. JOHN ACORN

4

GLENMORE RESERVOIR

'M AN EDMONTON boy, born and raised, but I do like Calgary, perhaps because I really don't care at all about hockey. So there I was, looking out over the remarkably blue waters (mountain stream water, not slough water) of the Glenmore Reservoir, from a high point in South Glenmore Park. A thousand or more Franklin's Gulls were hawking mayflies over the lake, and the cliffs of North Glenmore Park seemed particularly scenic on the opposite shore. To my right, the sternwheeler of Heritage Park was plying the waters, with the sound of a steam locomotive coming

◀ Northern Rough-winged Swallows nest in cliffsides, but not in large colonies. JOHN ACORN

But there are also additional habitats here, including the cliffsides and the Glenmore Pathway trail, which extends over a lovely pedestrian bridge spanning the Elbow River (with a tremendous Cliff Swallow colony on it) before continuing on into the Weaselhead.

GETTING THERE

To get to South Glenmore Park, take Hwy. 8 (Glenmore Trail) to 14th St. south, then 90th Ave. west, and down 24th St. to the parking lot. From there, simply walk over to the top of the bank and start birding. The Elbow River Pathway is well signed and should be immediately apparent.

North Glenmore Park is also accessible off Glenmore Trail. Take Crowchild Trail (the next major exit off Glenmore Trail to the west of the 14th St. exit) to the south, and follow it along until it becomes North Glenmore Park Rd. You'll have a choice of parking areas as you make your way to the west.

The Weaselhead Natural Area has an additional access point and parking area in the southwest corner of the Lakeview neighbourhood at 37th St. and 66th Ave.

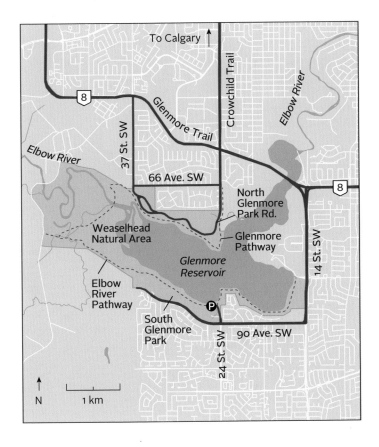

At the terminal, Gyrfalcons hunt pigeons almost every day in wintertime.
GERALD ROMANCHUK

5

ALBERTA GRAIN TERMINAL, EDMONTON

OR MANY, BIRDING is a connection with what they consider to be "nature." For others, it's a connection with birds. But what is nature, really? For birders in Edmonton, one of the most popular winter birding spots is about as *un*natural as you could imagine—the Alberta Grain Terminal. Built in 1924 by the federal government, the terminal has been loading grain into CN Rail cars ever since, and is now operated by Cargill. There have been internal renovations but the ancient exterior has been preserved. The south face of the building is the key to its bird appeal, with plenty of pipes, sills, and brackets for Rock Pigeons to roost on. On a sunny day in winter, the front of the building can be 10°C (about 18°F) warmer than its surroundings (I measured it with an infrared thermometer). It's not unusual to find a thousand pigeons on the building early in the morning, and shortly thereafter, the falcons show up. Those of us who frequent the terminal for birding once thought that its appeal was spilled grain for the pigeons, but after years of observation, it seems more likely that the terminal is, to pigeons, the ultimate cozy cliff face. When the pigeons sense danger, they all fly up at once, forming a huge, swirling mass that stays just to the south of the building.

Beginning almost 30 years ago, birder and railway worker Jim Lange noticed both Gyrfalcons and Prairie Falcons hunting pigeons at the terminal. Both species have been regulars ever since. On a good day, a birder might see a dozen or so predation attempts, but perhaps only a single successful hunt. My own observations confirm that the falcons have about a 10% success rate catching pigeons, although in a 2001 paper Dick Dekker and Jim Lange documented the habits of some particularly deadly Prairie Falcons that caught pigeons more than 26% of the time. It all happens more or less right overhead, so the wildlife photography crowd also loves the terminal. Everyone is hoping for the dramatic photograph of Gyrfalcon or Prairie Falcon, talons out, just before it grabs a fleeing pigeon. Some of the folks who frequent the place (I call them "the terminal cases") are more or less addicted to it (and yes, I'm one of them), while others come to see the falcons for their life list and leave satisfied after a single visit.

Along with the two big falcons, it's common to see Merlins at the terminal (although they very rarely catch pigeons), as well as the occasional Peregrine Falcon (very few overwinter here), Bald Eagle, or Northern Goshawk.

Rough-legged Hawks, Cooper's Hawks, Coyotes, and Red Foxes sometimes pass by as well. Every winter is different, as individual raptors make the terminal a regular part of their routine. Of course, Common Ravens are also abundant, and they often steal pigeons from the falcons. The falcons sometimes retaliate as well, even fatally. It's an intense spectacle, and who knows how long it will continue, what with the age of the building and the single public access point.

BIRDING GUIDE

You may have a great experience the moment you first arrive, but my advice is to plan to be patient and to spend some quality time working on your industrial aesthetic sense as you wait. Typically, you'll have lots of company, and the other birders will be happy to gossip about what's been happening among the falcons. Gyrfalcons generally arrive sometime in mid-November, and leave sometime in mid- to late-March. Prairie Falcons seem to follow about the same schedule, even though they now nest in the west end of Edmonton and could hunt at the terminal any time of year. Once they get into a routine, the falcons generally begin chasing the pigeons sometime after 10:30 a.m., and continue until about mid-afternoon. After that, you can sometimes see a falcon roosting on the terminal with a full crop and a full tummy, but hunts aren't common in late afternoon. The first Gyrfalcon to regularly use the terminal (a light-morph bird—subsequent ones have been grey) would roost on the building at night, but since then they've always flown away before sunset. Where they roost now is anyone's guess.

The main parking lot/viewing location is the place to go. Make sure not to trespass anywhere. It's important to keep relations between birders and the industrial neighbours good. CN Rail has its own security patrol, and the fenced compound between the parking lot and the railway is owned by the Edmonton Police Service—so behave. If you want other, although more distant, views of the terminal, you can park at the north end of 129 St., south of the tracks, or you can try the residential roads to the east of the terminal. Both might produce a roosting raptor. Elsewhere along the rail corridor, access is very limited. My advice is to be thankful for the parking lot and sit tight. You can also see the falcons at the terminal from Arby's on St. Albert Trail if you take your binoculars in with you.

GETTING THERE

To reach the best viewing area and parking space, first get onto the service road along the north side of the Yellowhead Trail, between St. Albert Trail and 129 St. If you're driving west on the Yellowhead, you can turn onto the (unmarked but obvious) service road at about 130 St., then turn left. Or if you're driving east, you can access the service road from St. Albert Trail. From the service road, the access road that leads to the parking area is located just west of about 130 St., roughly opposite the very obvious grain terminal itself, and marked by a sign that reads "13030-13044 Yellowhead Trail." Take this short road until you see a fenced compound to the right, and park in the area just south of the fence. Don't be tempted to park in the lot to the left, even though it's a bit closer to the terminal. It's police property, and they've asked the birders to stay out.

On the breeding grounds, many shorebirds, such as this Marbled Godwit, will sometimes perch in trees. JOHN ACORN

6

GULL LAKE

ENTRAL ALBERTA HAS fewer lakes than you might think, so each one is worth considering as a birding location. Gull is, quite honestly, my favourite, mostly because my mother's family has had a summer cabin there for about a century now. This is where I had not only my first birthday party but also many of my formative birding experiences. In fact, I'm typing these words in our cabin right now.

Gull is a big, shallow lake. The main change since the construction of the first summer cabins is that about half the lake has dried up. Oddly enough, this made it better for at least some birds. In the 1970s, along the south shore, the Summer Village used to rake the beach with a tractor, which allowed the loose sand to blow into a dune ridge, behind which Piping Plovers nested, much to my delight. The occasional Piping Plover still shows up, but only on migration. The exposed lakebed in front of the cabins became accreted

There are a few points of access on the west side of the lake, including a few public access points and the relatively recent Sandy Point development. The north end is less accessible, as is the east side of the lake, but a driving circuit around the lake will no doubt provide plenty of birding pleasure, at least once the ponds fill with waterfowl and the raptors return from the south.

GETTING THERE

Gull Lake is about equidistant from Edmonton and Calgary (about 150 km/100 mi.), about 15 km off Hwy. 2 via Hwy. 12 to the west. Take the well-marked turnoff at RR 282 to the Summer Village of Gull Lake, and watch for any of the eight paths (marked "Beach Path" or "Lake Access Route") along the main road in the village that parallel the lakeshore. At the west end of the village, Scott Dr. also takes you to the lakeshore, but this sand road is often bumpy and wet. West of the Summer Village, at Aspen Beach Provincial Park, a boardwalk over a marsh connects the Ebeling Day Use Area and the Brewers Campground to the Lakeview Campground. From the provincial park, proceed west on 50 Ave. toward Bentley to circumnavigate the lake. You can follow the signs north to Sandy Point on RR 11 and bird the recently developed beach area, or you can head west of Bentley to Hwy. 20 north, and soon thereafter, Hwy. 771. Take Westlake Rd. to the east to reach the Stoner's Landing Public Boat Launch. Alternatively, continue north on 771 and take Parkland Dr. to the Summer Village of Parkland Beach, where there's a public park along the lakeshore. Hwy. 771 runs north to meet Hwy. 53, which takes you east to Hwy. 792 (Woody Nook Rd.). Heading south on 792, take

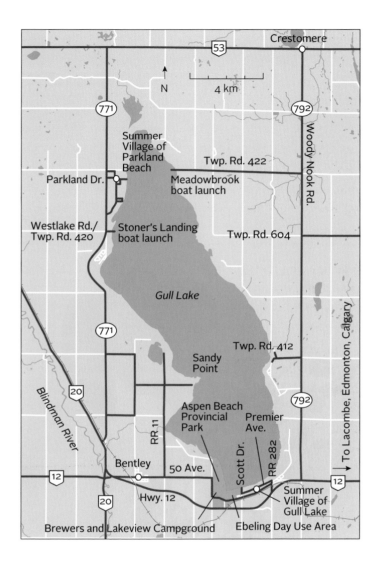

TWP Rd. 422 to the Meadowbrook Public Boat Launch, the only easy public access to the east side of the lake (although there's a public walking trail, which I haven't tried out, in the New Saratoga Beach development, at the west end of TWP Rd. 412).

Northern Goshawks can be quite defensive around a nest site.

GERALD ROMANCHUK

7

LAC LA BICHE

T HE BOREAL FOREST holds a special allure for birders. It's
the breeding place of untold millions of songbirds and
the last great wilderness on the North American continent. We often hear that it's also under threat, from oil
sands developments and other aspects of the ever-expand-
ing footprint of humanity. In reality, there's quite a bit of
diversity within the boreal, with respect to both birds and
threats, and as with any gigantic ecoregion, getting to know
the boreal is no simple matter. A great starting point, however, is Sir Winston Churchill Provincial Park, on Big Island
in the middle of Lac La Biche, just 2.5 hours from Edmonton.

Here, the forests are some 300 years old, protected from
fire by the waters of this gorgeous northern lake. The surrounding mainland burned extensively in the 1930s—and

is great birding country as well—but the Island is truly remarkable. How it's avoided going up in smoke, what with a continual flow of campers, hikers, and smokers since the park was connected to the mainland by a causeway in 1968, is anyone's guess. There are other beautiful examples of old-growth boreal forest in Alberta (at Cold Lake Provincial Park, for example), but Big Island is always at the top of my list.

I had my first summer job away from home here, as the park naturalist for the summers of 1977 and '78. I kept detailed field notes, and even now I marvel at the diversity of warblers and other songbirds that were lifers for me back then, not to mention the nesting Broad-winged Hawks, Northern Goshawks, and Osprey. I especially remember a visit from the Edmonton Bird Club. I joined them at the park gate early in the morning, and we set out with a particular goal in mind—to find a Cape May Warbler. Surrounded by singing Yellow-rumped, Mourning, Black-and-White, and even Blackburnian Warblers, we eventually found a Cape May. At that point, one of the birders announced that she was heading back to the phone booth to "call town." It seems that the two senior members of the club (Otto Hohn and Bob Lister) were allowed to sleep in and enjoy their coffee in their motel room in Lac La Biche. When they got the call, they rushed out to the park and were reverently guided to the Cape May's tree.

In recent years, I've been bringing my environmental science and forestry students here for the bird component of their spring field school. They love the forests, the birdsong (especially Winter Wrens), the Osprey and Bald Eagles on their nests, and the possibility of finding a Long-eared Owl, low down in the forests on the causeway island or the Long Point Trail.

BIRDING GUIDE

If you can, camp on the Island. From my tent trailer, I always hear a few species of birds around the campground that are tricky to find elsewhere. From the campground, it's easy to access the various walking trails through the 234 ha (580 acre) park and get down to the shoreline and the various beaches. Keep in mind, though, that outside camping season, the park roads may be closed to vehicle traffic, meaning you have to walk in from the park gate. This is not as onerous as it sounds, though, since even the forested traffic circle near the entrance is often loaded with warblers, creepers, and woodpeckers.

My favourite trails are the Boardwalk Trail (with very old mixed forests and some peatland) and the Long Point Trail (with great views of the lake and some odd vegetation such as an ancient pin-cherry forest). The interior trails (which were originally intended as firefighting access roads, but now have lovely names such as Kinglet Trail, Old Growth Alley, and Birch Snag Trail) are also great for birding, especially near the central firewood storage area, where the White Spruce and Balsam Poplar trees seem especially attractive to the less common species of warblers.

The main lake access points are at the Camper's Beach, the Day Use Beach, and the Pelican Islands Viewing Platform. Scan the water for loons, grebes, scoters, and other water birds, and watch for Osprey fishing along the shallows. On the Pelican Islands themselves, there's always something to see, especially if you have a good spotting scope. When I worked here in the 1970s, American White Pelicans and Double-crested Cormorants were considered rare and threatened, but nowadays these birds are common, and the big concern is the future of the walleye fishery in Lac La Biche. It's a superb spot, and about the only negative thing I can say about this lake is that it's not much for shorebirds. If you can live with that minor shortcoming, I think you'll love it here.

GETTING THERE

From Lac La Biche townsite, which is about 215 km (130 mi.) northeast of Edmonton, take the main street (101 Ave.) out of town to the northeast, where it becomes Hwy. 881. A few kilometres farther, turn west/left onto Provincial Park Rd. and follow it down to the park. It crosses a causeway, which runs through Long Island, before joining Big Island and the main body of the park. In terms of roads, the park layout is very simple. A rather large, forested "traffic circle" connects to a loop road, which runs all the way around the park. If you take the loop road counter-clockwise, you quickly reach the Day Use Area to the northeast, where a smaller loop takes you to a number of picnic sites and a beach. Past that, there's a turnoff to the right with parking for both the Old Growth Alley Trail and the Pelican Islands Viewpoint. The next stop area along the loop is a parking area for the Long Point and Boardwalk Trails. Then there's the Lac La Biche Lookout, on a height of land, and also the campground, with its own beach parking lot, and a concession/shower building. A group camping area, between the main campground

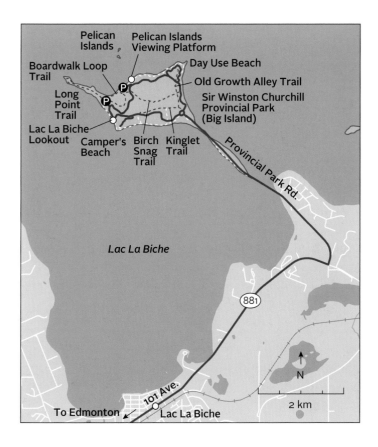

and the park entrance, provides another access point to the lake. The trail system is much like the road system, in that it's based on a big loop, but there are more interconnecting trails criss-crossing the islands' interior, as well as the Long Point Trail, extending out along the Long Point peninsula to the northwest.

Western Kingbirds are among the many songbirds that brighten up the campground. JOHN ACORN

8

LAKE NEWELL

I T'S ALL "ARTIFICIAL," but the birds don't care, and therefore neither should you. Lake Newell is an irrigation reservoir (its original name was the Lake Newell Reservoir),
created in 1914, and its main attraction, Kinbrook Island
Provincial Park, was established in 1951, complete with
extensive ornamental plantings, cottages, and a whole lot
of manicured lawn. Seeing the opportunity for waterfowl
enhancement, Ducks Unlimited and other agencies then
built wetlands adjacent to the east of the lake to promote
duck breeding. The whole shebang is an irresistible draw
for a whole variety of birds, situated as it is in the middle of
open prairie rangeland and biologically monotonous crops.

Most of the trees in the campground areas are cottonwoods, so birds that regularly use the riparian cottonwood
forests along the big prairie rivers, such as the Red Deer and

empties into the lake over a weir, birding is quite good. As you drive around, you also have a shot at a variety of grassland species, such as Loggerhead Shrike, Long-billed Curlew, and Sprague's Pipit.

GETTING THERE

Lake Newell is directly south of Brooks, and Kinbrook Island is about a 16 km (10 mi.) drive south from the Trans-Canada Hwy. on Hwy. 873 and then TWP Rd. 173A, which ends in a short causeway between two sections of marsh. The campground at the park is divided into three sections: the north section near the boat launch, the south section near the cottage area (the best area for songbirds), and the group camping area to the southeast, accessible via a causeway. The trailhead for the Kinbrook Marsh Nature Trail is at the end of a short gravel road leading north from the east end of the entrance road causeway. Watch for rather understated signage for the trail itself, contrasting with the high-budget panels that explain the history of the constructed marshes.

To get to the south end of the lake, return to Hwy. 873 and travel south a bit more than 3 km (1.8 mi.), until the road curves to the west. The dirt trails will be off to your right, and the road along the berm makes its way north and through a network of well sites, returning east to the highway about a kilometre south of the park turnoff.

To get to the Lake Newell Resort, go north on Hwy. 873 to TWP Rd. 182, and follow along to the west, turning south onto Lake Newell Resort Rd., which leads through the development and over the weir.

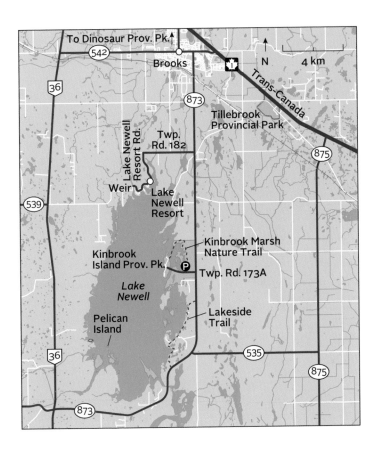

9

PAKOWKI LAKE

OR BIRDERS IN Alberta, Pakowki Lake has long held
a mystique as a window into that biodiverse wonder-
land to the south, the place we call Montana. Pakowki
was the first place in Alberta where one could reliably
find White-faced Ibis (they were originally misidentified
as Glossy Ibis, a very similar species that was recently con-
firmed at Pakowki in 2017, and is also expanding its range),
not to mention Black-necked Stilt and the occasional Great
or Snowy Egret. Nowadays, these species (well, maybe not
the Snowy Egret) are just as likely to turn up well to the
north into the parklands, but a few years back, Pakowki

◄ Burrowing Owls are increasingly rare, but still regular near Pakowki Lake.
GERALD ROMANCHUK

produced a Black-headed Gull, a vagrant from Europe, and the lure of the lake was restored. You really never know what you'll find here, and although that same statement could be applied anywhere, really, the proximity of Pakowki to the southern border of the province, combined with the fact that it's a relatively isolated water body, makes it all the more likely that it will attract the rarities. Pakowki is shallow, but deep enough to hold fish, including pike. When conditions are dry, it shrinks down to a tiny and relatively salty bathtub, and the rest of the lakebed becomes a grassy meadow. When rain is plentiful, as happens in some years, the lake fills with water, and on the map it becomes as large as any other lake mentioned in the Alberta section of this book. With these changes, and changes to other aspects of the vegetation, come changes in the birdlife. The lake goes from being a quiet meadow to being a noisy marsh. In late summer, Pakowki Lake can also occasionally be the site of botulism poisoning of waterfowl, an unfortunate event that is no less disturbing on account of its naturalness. On my first visit to Pakowki, with my friend Nancy Baron, in 1980, dead and dying waterfowl surrounded us. I'm happy to report that I haven't seen anything quite as dramatic here since, although a summer visit will usually turn up one or two afflicted ducks.

BIRDING GUIDE

Access to the lake is limited, since most of the roads that approach the lake lead to farms. The western arm of Pakowki is the classic birding spot. Once you arrive, find a place where you can park off the road (but don't block the farmers' access to their pastures) and walk along the causeway. Or, you can drive along the causeway slowly, using your vehicle as a blind. Scan carefully, watching for rarities such as the occasional Clark's Grebe among the more abundant Western Grebes. The only other easy access to the lake is on the south end, but this area is often dry. Nonetheless, I like to drive around the lake, since the ranchlands in this corner of the province are full of prairie birds. In summer, I almost always find at least one Loggerhead Shrike and Prairie Falcon, and the area is also good for such species as Chestnut-collared Longspur, McCown's Longspur, and Lark Bunting. If you're lucky, you might even find a Burrowing Owl, and during migration, you might see a Smith's Longspur. Traffic is sparse around Pakowki, and you may find that some of the locals enjoy chatting with you about the birds they've seen. For a slice of pie at the nicest small-town museum in Alberta, and interesting conversation about the area, I recommend a visit to Etzikom.

I should also mention that Pakowki Lake isn't quite far enough east for Greater Sage-Grouse, but they're only a short drive away (the area southeast of Manyberries is where the few remaining birds live now). On the way to or from Pakowki, however, you might want to stop at Red Rock Coulee (just off Hwy. 887, north of Orion), for the spectacular concretions and the great vista. It's also a good location for Rock Wrens and Common Nighthawks.

GETTING THERE

Pakowki Lake lies south of Hwy. 1 and the South Saskatchewan River. I usually take Hwy. 3 for about 40 km (25 mi.)

southwest from Medicine Hat, and then Hwy. 885 to
Etzikom and the west end of the lake (another 60 km). South
of the west arm, Hwy. 885 is good for prairie birds, and it
intersects Hwy. 501, which cuts across the south arm of Pakowki not far to the east. This section of highway has been
good for raptors in the past. On the east side of the lake, take
Hwy. 887 north to Orion, watching for shrikes and other
prairie species, and then, if you like, complete the loop by
driving west on Hwy. 61 back to Etzikom.

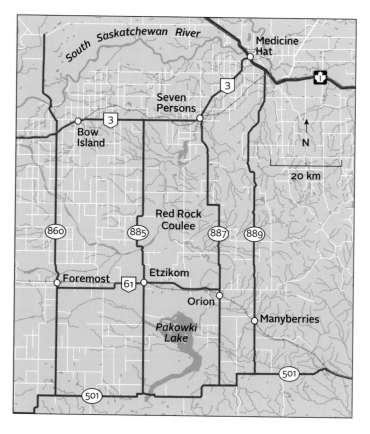

—10—

WABAMUN LAKE

OR A BIG birdy lake only a short distance from Edmonton, Wabamun Lake is commonly but understandably underrated. Prior to 2010, the coal-fired Wabamun Generating Station dumped warm water directly into the lake year-round, affecting water quality and giving the lake a polluted image, heightened by the surrounding open-pit coal mines and the stacks on all three power plants in the area. In 2005, a CN freight train derailed and spilled 800,000 litres (210,000 gallons) of heavy oil into the lake, killing a large number of water birds, especially Western and Red-necked Grebes, and restricting the fishery to catch-and-release ever since. To this day, most Edmontonians think of Lac Ste. Anne, to the north, as the more pristine destination.

However, Wabamun also has a long and proud history as a birding destination. For a long time, Edmonton birders

The best Alberta rednecks are all Red-necked Grebes.
JOHN ACORN

focused on the magnificence of Beaverhills Lake, an equal distance to the east of the city, but these days Beaverhills has all but dried up, and it's time to look to the west. Things change, and just as the anglers have discovered that the fishing in Wabamun is now better than ever before (catch-and-release regulations were just what the fishery needed), it's time for birders to realize that Wabamun is also superb—and getting better all the time.

Wabamun is great for water birds, as well as raptors and passerines. Numerous pairs of Osprey nest in the area, and Bald Eagles also nest and forage around the lake and, in winter, near the cooling ponds. A wide variety of water birds have brightened the day for birders over the years, including all three scoter species, Yellow-billed and Pacific Loons, and Trumpeter Swans. Recreational boaters crowd the lake in summertime, but luckily the birding is best in the spring and fall, so you can avoid annoyance by finding quieter spots between the May long weekend and Labour Day. One such nearby spot is Hasse Lake, a particularly birdy location thanks to a low, gravelly island used for breeding and roosting by hundreds of Ring-billed Gulls, other gulls, pelicans, cormorants, and waterfowl. And yes, do give Lac Ste. Anne a look as well, especially during the open water season. But note that it's not very birdy in wintertime.

BIRDING GUIDE

From Edmonton, I like to head all the way to Seba Beach to check the town for passerines and grouse in wintertime and water birds in summer. Likewise, I travel south and east around the lake in wintertime and back along the north side in summer.

Winter birding at Wabamun is a combination of town and feeder birding, the occasional and unpredictable owl or shrike, and waterfowl on open water at the power plants. For feeders, look in the town of Wabamun, Seba Beach, and any of the various small cottage developments around the lake. If winter owls and shrikes are your focus, remember that they're irruptive, appearing everywhere in some years, nowhere in others, and anywhere in most. As for water birds, the cooling pond and canal of the Sundance Power Plant aren't terribly easy to access, but if you park carefully, off the road, you can clamber up to the fence by the side of Sundance Rd. and peer out over the water. Access is granted to Christmas Bird Count participants, but birders shouldn't expect the TransAlta power company to accommodate them at other times, and certainly shouldn't trespass. At the Keephills Plant you can scan the canal and part of the cooling pond from beside the hilltop graveyard just east of the plant, and with permission from TransAlta (call them first: 403-267-7110) you can access the pond on the east side, keeping in mind that both anglers and waterfowl hunters also use this area. This is a great spot for Bald Eagles in wintertime, as well as the occasional Golden Eagle and Gyrfalcon.

In summer, when water birds are the focus, plan to look west over the water in the morning and east in the afternoon, to keep the sun at your back. The best vista on the west end is in the town of Seba Beach, while the best spots on the east are at the provincial park and the Ironhead Golf Course, where you can access the lake near the parking lot. On the north side, there are access points in Wabamun itself (although the town park now charges $20 per day for parking in summer), as well as at Fallis and a few other cottage developments (but watch for No Parking signs). On the south side, most of the cottage areas do allow at least one access point. For woodland birds, the best trails are at Wabamun Provincial Park, but there are good roadside woods all around the lake.

GETTING THERE

It takes less than an hour to get to Wabamun Lake from Edmonton, via Hwy. 16 (70 km/45 mi.). You can turn south from the highway at RR 35 to reach Wabamun Lake Provincial Park and the Ironhead Golf Course, RR 40B to reach the town of Wabamun, RR 52 to reach Fallis, or Hwy. 31 to reach Seba Beach. Fallis and Wabamun are connected by Lakeshore Rd., which also connects to Hwy. 16 via RR 43 and RR 44.

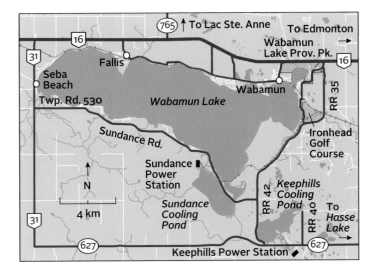

To access the south side of the lake, take Hwy. 31 south from Seba Beach, and turn east on TWP Rd. 530. This road becomes Sundance Rd., and it winds its way to RR 42, where you can turn north to rejoin Hwy. 16, or south to Hwy. 627, which leads east to the Keephills Plant and the cooling pond that's accessible via RR 40.

To get to Hasse Lake, make your way to the north-south Hwy. 770, via either Hwy. 16 or Hwy. 627, and turn east toward the park on TWP Rd. 524, following the signs after that. Lac Ste. Anne is north of Wabamun Lake, accessible from Hwy. 765 or Hwy. 43.

Great Blue Herons are relatively common, but always spectacular.

GERALD ROMANCHUK

—11—

WEED LAKE

ONCE UPON A time, Weed Lake, quite near the town of Langdon (not to be confused with the Langdon Reservoir), was a lake. Then, in 1971, it was drained to make room for farmland. And then, in 2006, Ducks Unlimited, along with some of its partners, refilled the lake for the sake of waterfowl and other birds. The result was a spectacular birding site within easy reach of Calgary.

In some ways, Weed Lake is much like any other shallow prairie water body, but experienced birders quickly realize that each such lake has a slightly different mix of birds, and that this mix might change from day to day. A spotting scope will help when birding this spot, since many of the birds will be quite distant. Much of the fun in a place like this comes from scanning the water for rarities and rescanning, since many birds dive or hide among the reeds. With so many birds on it during the peak season, there's always going to be something interesting out on the water. Perhaps it will be a Trumpeter Swan, a Great Blue Heron, or an interesting shorebird. Although the lake is primarily managed for ducks, the shorebird habitat here is fantastic. Few species nest at Weed Lake, but you could see just about any Alberta shorebird during migration, which begins in earnest in May and resumes in July when the first of the Arctic migrants begin to return south.

Photographers will enjoy this spot as well, perhaps not so much for the sake of close-up water bird photos (the Frank Lake blind is much better (see page 22), but you might get lucky at Weed Lake too) but for the fact that you never know what might fly past as you settle into one of the access points. The farmland around the lake can also be quite photogenic.

Nearby, the Langdon Corner Slough is a great place for shorebirds, with more American Avocets than I've ever seen at a single location. These birds also breed here. The slough also contains a grassy island, complete with fake palm trees. There, a number of birds both nest and roost, and not long ago many birders were treated to a very regular Arctic Tern at the island. I really hope the palm trees persist—they're a quirky reminder that everything here is, on the one hand, ridiculously artificial, but on the other, entirely to the liking of a huge variety of wild creatures.

Of course, the surrounding area is also good for terrestrial birds, and you should keep a sharp eye out for a variety of sparrows, other passerines, and the occasional raptor. For classic prairie birding, you'll have to go farther east and south, but for Calgary area open-country birds, this is a fine spot indeed.

BIRDING GUIDE

Weed Lake is primarily a spring and summer destination, shared with hunters in the fall. Arriving at the lake, take note of where the birds are and where the sun is, since birding is much easier with birds close in front of you and the sun at your back. Then strike a compromise between the two. The south access is great, but when the birding is good, the two-vehicle parking spot may be full. Don't be tempted to park at nearby farm access points, since the landowners will quickly evict you (or so I've been told). The east access is served by a good road and has ample parking at the end. You can scope the lake from here, or walk through the gate and alongside the marsh and canal to the south, then west to the lake where the Jerry Brunen Uplands provide a great observation point. From here, you can see the access on the west side, which may be very muddy if not impassable when wet, but is very good for birding when dry. The north access is rather distant from the lake, but with a scope you might spot some interesting birds, however backlit. While at Weed Lake, be sure to check out the Langdon Corner Slough as well, with plenty of great shorebird habitats, and more waterfowl, terns, and gulls.

GETTING THERE

Weed Lake is only a short distance (35 km/22 mi.) east of Calgary, just northeast of the town of Langdon, and south of the Trans-Canada Hwy. on Hwy. 797 where it intersects with Hwy. 560, the eastern extension of Glenmore Trail.

On Weed Lake itself, there are four access points. The two on the east and west sides (both via TWP Rd. 240) are the best, although the east access has a much better road (which leads west from RR 270, Boundary Rd.). The south access point is about 1.7 km (1 mi.) east of Hwy. 797 on Hwy. 560. There's room for only two vehicles at the locked gate with the Weed Lake sign, but there's a nice foot access area beyond the gate. The north viewpoint is at the end of the service road leading from Hwy. 797 east, south of the Trans-Canada. To the west, this same service road leads to the north end of the Langdon Corner Slough, and you can park along the paved roadside and glass the slough from there.

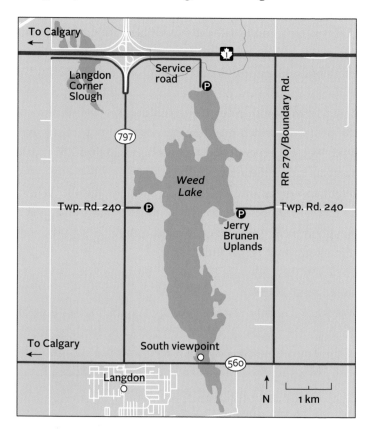

A wary female Common Merganser passes below one of the many pedestrian bridges over the Whitemud Creek. JOHN ACORN

12

WHITEMUD RAVINE

OBERT KROETSCH WROTE in his 1968 book *Alberta*, "Whitemud Park preserves the only major Edmonton ravine that hasn't become a highway: its forest and prairie cover is still home to such rare birds as the barred owl, the red-tailed hawk, and the pileated woodpecker." That was 50 years ago, and it's still true today, minus the puzzling reference to "prairie." I think of Whitemud Ravine as a vein of old-growth boreal forest, tucked into the folds of a major city, and although there are other, smaller ravines in town, and the almost-as-nice Mill Creek Ravine, Whitemud is the pride of Edmonton's naturalist community. Within it,

◄ A walk in Whitemud Ravine is always considered successful when you see a Brown Creeper. GERALD ROMANCHUK

Whitemud Creek itself flows freely and serves as a spawning stream for fish and as habitat for such bird species as Common Merganser and Belted Kingfisher.

As for rare birds, Barred Owls continue to surprise and delight the birding and hiking crowd (as do Great Horned and Northern Saw-whet Owls), but I would venture that Red-tailed Hawks and Pileated Woodpeckers are much more common now than they were half a century ago. Today, birders are more likely to prowl the ravine in search of Black-backed Woodpeckers, Brown Creepers, and Northern Goshawks, at least in wintertime. During spring migration and the breeding season, the crowd-pleasing species include Western Tanager, Northern Rough-winged Swallow, and a good variety of wood warblers. Over the years, an assortment of true rarities have appeared here, including Harlequin Duck and Hooded Warbler, just to mention those that begin with an *H*.

When I first began visiting the ravine (I grew up across the river, in Laurier Heights), all of the trails were foot trails, and the place had a wonderfully wild feel to it. Now, the lower sections of the ravine at least have wide, well-maintained trails that are fortunately off-limits to bicycles and off-leash dogs. It's common to meet people with binoculars or long telephoto lenses here. I take my wildlife biology students to the ravine for a field trip every March, and nothing makes me happier than to meet on the trail a former student who has returned for another look.

BIRDING GUIDE

If you're thinking of a short walk—one to three hours— begin by choosing one of three stretches of the ravine. The northern stretch extends from the Rainbow Valley ski area downstream to the mouth of Whitemud Creek, just east of the Quesnell Bridge over the North Saskatchewan River. This is the most accessible section of the ravine, and the trails here are carefully tended by the city. Watch for any of the birds mentioned above in the very old White Spruce and Balsam Poplar forest, as well as in and along the creek itself. Some of the regular hikers put out birdseed, and consequently, many of the chickadees and nuthatches along the trail are ridiculously tame. I generally keep to the main trail, although I also make a habit of visiting the hillside just south of the toboggan hill beside the Alfred H. Savage Centre. There, a few spring-fed seeps will sometimes attract American Robins in winter, as well as serving as bathing spots for a variety of other birds, at least on sunny days.

The middle stretch of the ravine runs between 23 Ave. in the south and Whitemud Dr. in the north. Here, the trails are also well maintained, and although the birdlife is much like that of the northern stretch, I recommend both with equal enthusiasm. Lately, the middle stretch has been particularly good for Barred Owls. A number of trails connect to the neighbourhoods east and west of this area. Note that, unlike the northern stretch, the trail system here can be confusing for first-time visitors.

The southern stretch of the ravine is less developed and so, for many people, more inviting. It consists of the northern Larch Sanctuary and the southern Mactaggart Sanctuary. It runs from the Anthony Henday Trail in the south to 23 Ave. in the north. Here, the trails are maintained only by the actions of human feet, and as a result they're "lower impact" than the over-engineered trails elsewhere along the ravine. Birdlife here is abundant and varied, and a few lovely oxbow ponds create habitats that are not seen along the other two stretches. As well, the Whitemud Creek is joined here by Blackmud Creek from the southeast. Both are worth exploring. I consider the southern stretch to end at Anthony Henday Dr., but the valley of the Whitemud Creek extends farther south and into the rapidly converted farmlands toward the airport.

Birding in Whitemud is good year-round. In winter, it's one of the best locations in the city. At other times, it's a nearby, and very welcome, reminder of the great forests to the north and west of Edmonton.

GETTING THERE

To get to the northern stretch, I usually park anywhere in the picnic and tobogganing area, accessible by taking Whitemud Dr. to Fox Dr. and then turning north (left) onto Keillor Rd. To get to the southern end of this stretch, turn south off Whitemud Dr. onto 122 St., and then west on Rainbow Valley Rd. to the parking area near the ski hill. It's also possible to access the northern stretch from trails off 53 Ave. on the west side, and the southwest corner of the University of Alberta Farm on the east side.

Parking for the middle stretch is best on the south side of Whitemud Dr., just off Rainbow Valley Rd., although this small parking lot can often fill up with dog walkers, making it necessary to park at Rainbow Valley. At the south end of the middle stretch, there's another parking lot on the south side of 23 Ave. Trails from the neighbourhoods are too numerous to mention here. My only advice is to leave a trail of breadcrumbs so you can find your way back to the car.

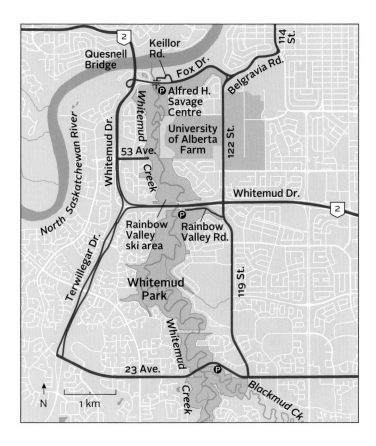

For the southern stretch (now designated the "Larch Sanctuary"), you really only have one easy choice for a parking lot, the spot on the south side of 23 Ave. There's no easy access at Anthony Henday Dr., or along Ellerslie Rd. to the south of it.

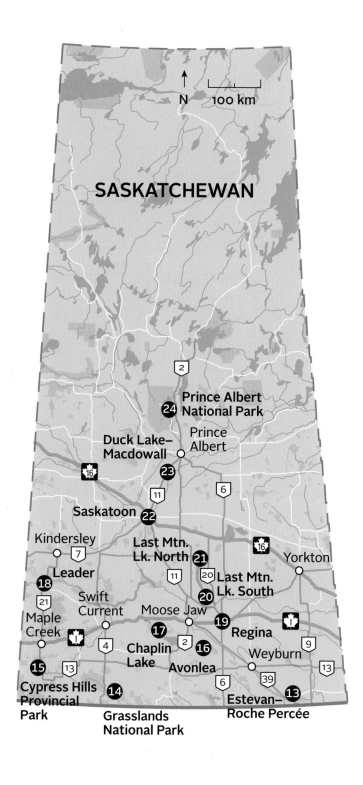

N   100 km

SASKATCHEWAN

2

24 Prince Albert
National Park

Duck Lake–   Prince
Macdowall   Albert

16

23

11

Saskatoon 22

6

Kindersley
        7

Last Mtn.
Lk. North   21   16   Yorkton

18   20 Last Mtn.
Leader   Lk. South
        21   11
Swift   20
Maple   Current Moose Jaw
Creek   19
        1   17   Regina
        4   Chaplin   2 16
15   13   Lake   Avonlea   Weyburn
                                    6   39   13
        14   Estevan–
Cypress Hills   13
Provincial   Grasslands   Roche Percée
Park   National Park

9

13

SASKATCHEWAN

ALAN SMITH

Male Dickcissels are often seen singing from dock plants.

NICK SAUNDERS

−13−
ESTEVAN–
ROCHE PERCÉE

NOWN AS THE "Energy Capital" of Saskatchewan, Estevan lies in the midst of coal strip mines, and oil and gas
fields. The extraction of these minerals has had a pro-
found effect on the landscape of the region. Strip mining
for coal, in particular, has had a dramatic impact. Spoil piles
dominate much of the land on either side of the Souris River.
The river valley itself has been much altered by the Rafferty
Dam, whose reservoir extends from just west of Estevan
northwest toward Weyburn, and by Dutch elm disease,
which has killed most of the American Elms that formed
much of the woodland on the flood plain below Estevan.
Fortunately, the area still abounds in wildlife; much of it is
characteristic of the eastern deciduous forest and found only
in this corner of the province. Among its specialties are the

Canada Plum, Snapping Turtle, Eastern Fox Squirrel, and Eastern Cottontail, as well as several birds mentioned below. This site is at its best in the late spring and summer.

In spite of the day and night noises associated with the industrial activity, and the absolute tragedy of losing our elm forests, I've always enjoyed visiting the area. I guess it's the prospect of seeing some of those eastern specialties that keeps me coming back. Also of great interest to me as a biogeographer is the overlap of several closely related pairs of species—Western and Eastern Wood-Pewees, Say's and Eastern Phoebes, Lazuli and Indigo Buntings, Spotted and Eastern Towhees, and Black-headed and Rose-breasted Grosbeaks—in the area. One of my most memorable visits was on June 24, 1989, when I walked 23 km (14 mi.) from Roche Percée Campground to Estevan. I saw male Rose-breasted and Black-headed Grosbeaks in the same tree. I also heard a Field Sparrow and saw a Least Tern—more than enough reward for sunburned legs!

BIRDING GUIDE

On your way toward North Portal you may want to stop at the spoil piles to listen for Rock Wrens and check isolated trees for Ferruginous Hawk nests, or you may prefer to move more quickly to catch the dawn chorus along the Souris at the former Roche Percée Provincial Recreation Site. You'll probably have to park at the gate and walk, but it's only about 300 m/yds and it will be worth it. In the summer, the woods are alive with woodland birds such as the Veery, Black-and-white Warbler, and American Redstart. The ford across the Souris River is a good place for Lazuli Bunting and Yellow-breasted Chat. Other uncommon birds recorded in the area include the Black-headed and Rose-breasted Grosbeaks, and Yellow-throated Vireo. Check the river and oxbows here and elsewhere for Wood Duck and Hooded Merganser. From here, head to Roche Percée, a small village on the south bank of the Souris River. Listen along the road for Field Sparrows, an area specialty. Check any towhee you might see singing from the top of a shrub—although most will be Spotted Towhees, some will be Eastern Towhees. The road passes by two small oxbows of the Souris River, which are good for marsh-nesting birds.

Roche Percée is named for a pierced rock formation on the southern edge of the village. One of many in the area, the rock formation is a chronicle of the history of the area. First Nations peoples carved numerous petroglyphs in the soft sandstone, and European visitors from surveyors of the international boundary in 1873 and an RCMP detachment in 1874 to "Kilroys" of today have carved their initials in the yielding rock. Birding in and around the village can be rewarding. There is a huge Cliff Swallow colony under the railway overpass northwest of the village, and Lazuli Buntings, even the odd Indigo Bunting, and Rock Wrens can often be heard where the railway bridge crosses the Souris. This is one of the few areas (Avonlea is another) in Saskatchewan where you can expect to find Eastern and Say's Phoebes nesting in close proximity.

Running west from Roche Percée along the south bank of the Souris is TWP Rd. 14. Listen for Eastern Wood-Pewee and watch for Eastern Bluebird. After driving 3.5 km (2.2 mi.), turn south along RR 72 for 5 km, then turn west onto TWP Rd. 11, an area known for its nesting Dickcissels.

14

GRASSLANDS NATIONAL PARK: WEST BLOCK

GRASSLANDS NATIONAL PARK consists of two units: the West Block just east of Val Marie and the East Block west of Killdeer. The park's interpretive centre is located in Val Marie at the junction of Hwy. 4 and Centre St. The West Block includes the valley of the Frenchman River. The western portion of the West block was acquired decades ago and has good roads as well as many hiking trails and other amenities; the eastern part was only acquired in 2010, so road and trail access and amenities are limited as yet.

◄ McCown's Longspurs are not uncommon in the uplands of the national park and surrounding areas. NICK SAUNDERS¹

Sage-Grouse persist in the valley. Winter birding can also be good. Watch for Gray-crowned Rosy-Finch and a variety of raptors, especially Golden Eagle. On December 16, 1988, the late Wayne Harris, a top Saskatchewan biologist, saw all five species of Canadian falcons in and around the park! There are a few records of Common Poorwill, but these are from the eastern, recently added portions of the West Block. One of the few Saskatchewan breeding records of Sage Thrasher comes from lower Otter Creek, the second-last tributary to the Frenchman before it crosses the International Boundary.

I would recommend leaving the tour loop to travel east along the south side of the Frenchman, cross the bridge over the river, and turn left and drive toward the park boundary (this road eventually leads to Mankota and the West Block). This stretch of road has several large Black-tailed Prairie Dog colonies. It also takes you to the uplands, which offer another opportunity to see more longspurs, pipits, and Baird's Sparrows. After looping back to the Scenic Drive, you soon leave the valley and the park. The southern portion of the Scenic Drive is a good area to see Ferruginous Hawk and Long-billed Curlew—both species are more common in areas with a mix of farmland and grassland than unbroken grassland. Note that any hawk sitting on the ground is almost certain to be a "Ferrugie." Seventy Mile Butte, which is just south of Val Marie, is a good place to see Rock Wren.

GETTING THERE

Val Marie and the West Block of Grasslands National Park may be reached via Hwy. 4 (south) from Swift Current and

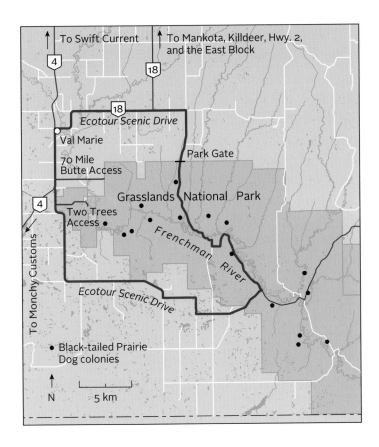

The following labels appear on the map:

↑ To Swift Current ↑ To Mankota, Killdeer, Hwy. 2, and the East Block

4

18

18
Ecotour Scenic Drive

Val Marie

Park Gate

70 Mile
Butte Access

Grasslands National Park

4

Two Trees
Access

Frenchman River

To Monchy Customs

Ecotour Scenic Drive

Black-tailed Prairie
Dog colonies

↑
N   5 km

the Trans-Canada Hwy. From Val Marie, take the Ecotour
Scenic Drive. To reach the Ecotour, from Hwy. 4 turn east
onto Hwy. 18. Drive east for 15 km (9.3 mi.), at which point
the highway turns north while the Scenic Drive turns south
into Grasslands National Park. Just before returning to
Hwy. 4 from the tour loop, you can reach the park at two
other sites: Two Trees Access, and also after you reach the
highway at 70 Mile Butte. The East Block is centred on the
Killdeer Badlands and may be reached via Hwy. 2 west of
the village of Killdeer. Hwy. 18 connects Val Marie and Killdeer and gives access to the two blocks.

15

CYPRESS HILLS INTERPROVINCIAL PARK: CENTRE BLOCK

THE CYPRESS HILLS are unique in Saskatchewan. As outliers of the Rocky Mountains, they share much of their flora and fauna with the mountains. The hills are actually a plateau, with sides vegetated by White Spruce, Lodgepole Pine, and Trembling Aspen and a tableland covered by fescue prairie. The last major fire was in 1870, and so many trees are well over a century old.

Cypress Hills Interprovincial Park is composed of two units covering most of the West and Centre Blocks of the Cypress Hills. The Gap Rd. connects the West and Centre Blocks. Note that side roads, including the Gap Rd., may

◄ The cheery song of the MacGillivray's Warbler may be heard in shrubby areas throughout the park. NICK SAUNDERS

become impassable when wet. Most of the human activity in the park is in the Centre Block and is concentrated around two small, artificial lakes: Loch Leven and Loch Lomond. Facilities include the park headquarters, campgrounds, and numerous related services and recreational facilities, along with private cottages. An excellent map of the core area is available at the park gate, and bird checklists and interpretive programs may be obtained at the nature centre.

The Centre Block is one of my favourite birding areas in the province and has been very good to me over the years, affording me several rarities, including Western Screech-Owl, Lewis's Woodpecker, Black-throated Gray Warbler, and Indigo Bunting—the last two the first records for the hills. From 1992 to 2014, I had a study area of around 250 sections centred on the town of Maple Creek (27 km/17 mi. to the north) where I would survey Ferruginous Hawks, usually checking around 50 sites, of which at least 20 were active in any given year—one of the highest densities in North America. This was in late June, and it was almost always hot! The antidote was to head to the hills to cool down. One big treat was the absence of mosquitoes—a common characteristic of the hills and other well-drained mountainous areas.

BIRDING GUIDE

The Cypress Hills are noted for bird species that nest nowhere else in the province, including Red-naped Sapsucker, Dusky Flycatcher, and MacGillivray's Warbler, and mountain races of several other species, including the Red-shafted race of Northern Flicker, Western Warbling Vireo, Audubon's Warbler, Pink-sided Junco, and the Bendire's race of Red Crossbill—all of which could one day be elevated to full species status. Although Common Poorwills perhaps also nest elsewhere, the Cypress Hills (especially the West Block) are their stronghold, and while Wild Turkeys were widely introduced in the province, the hills down to Maple Creek are the only area where they've persisted. Another specialty is the Townsend's Solitaire, which occurs in the non-breeding season throughout the southern half of the province, but is known to breed only in the hills. It appears the Pacific Wren can now be added to the list, as it's been found breeding since 2011 and even occasionally wintering in the hills. Many other mountain species of adjacent Alberta and Montana have been recorded on at least a few occasions since the late 1980s. These include Clark's Nutcracker, Mountain Chickadee, American Dipper, Townsend's Warbler (which has bred in the West Block at least once), and Cassin's Finch. "Solitary-type" vireos should be checked for either Cassin's or Plumbeous Vireo. Birding is best here in May to July, but winter birders can still be rewarded with American Three-toed Woodpecker, Townsend's Solitaire (as mentioned above), and both Red and White-winged Crossbills.

Three nature trails in the core area of the Centre Block provide good early morning birding. The best of these is the Highland Rotary Trail. The trailhead may be reached by turning left just past the entry park gate onto Ben Vannoch Dr. and driving until you reach the turnoff to the Lone Pine Group Campground and the trailhead. There's a map of the trail area at the parking lot showing a counter-clockwise walking loop 1.5 km (0.9 mi.) long that follows the shores of two beaver ponds.

GETTING THERE

The Centre Block of Cypress Hills Provincial Park is easily reached from the Trans-Canada Hwy. Simply turn south onto Hwy. 21 and drive 10 km (6 mi.) to Maple Creek and another 27 km to the junction with Hwy. 221. Drive 3.7 km down this short access highway, which leads west to the park gate and core area.

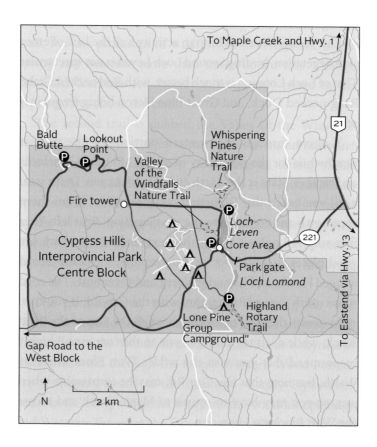

16

AVONLEA

A VONLEA IS A village situated on the boundary between the Regina Plains and the Missouri Coteau. Only 80 km (50 mi.) from the cities of Regina and Moose Jaw, it offers the birders living in or visiting these cities their closest opportunity to see most of the grassland and badland species characteristic of southern Saskatchewan. As is typical of the prairies, birding is best from spring to fall. Wooded areas include riparian woodlands along Avonlea Creek, on the north-facing slopes of the Dirt Hills (locals much prefer to use the name Blue Hills), and along intermittent creeks draining the hills; sites in general are all dominated by Green Ash. Badlands are found in the Avonlea Badlands and at the Claybank Brick Plant National Historical Site (henceforth the Brick Plant). Grasslands are found mainly east of Avonlea or in the Dirt Hills.

The ringing song of the Rock Wren may be heard both in the Avonlea Badlands and in the old clay mines at the Brick Plant. NICK SAUNDERS

After I retired in 2007, I moved to Avonlea with my significant other, Randi Edmonds. Although I'd spent most of my life in the city, the idea of Avonlea appealed to me, as I'd be living within miles of my favourite group of birds—the prairie birds. As a "city slicker," it took some getting used to rural life. If someone was seen entering a house, it was to leave something—like an apple pie—rather than to take something. The closest thing to a traffic jam was two farmers in half-ton trucks parked in opposite directions "chewing the fat." If you don't have CAA, you can get towed out for 12-pack of beer. All good!

BIRDING GUIDE

On your way from Regina or Moose Jaw, keep your eyes peeled for Rough-legged Hawks and Snowy Owls in the winter and Red-tailed Hawks in the fall on power poles, and Upland Sandpipers in the summer balancing awkwardly and precariously on the power lines. As you near Avonlea, a check at any farmstead or shelterbelt should yield an Orchard Oriole, and in tent caterpillar years, Black-billed Cuckoo. From Regina, you'll see a sign on Hwy. 334 for Grid 623 for Rouleau (famous as the site of Dog River in the TV series *Corner Gas*). But instead of heading north to Rouleau, turn south/left onto a dirt trail. Be cautious if it's rained recently as the trail becomes impassable when it's wet. A good tip here—and elsewhere, in fact—is if there are no tracks on the road, don't go! If it's passable you should see a lot of grassland birds along the right-hand side of the road. A pair of Ferruginous Hawks often nest in the large willow tree only 100 m/yds down the road. Farther down you

willow-ringed pond near the Bunkhouse is a good place for Willow Flycatcher and Yellow Warbler. If you go north beyond the Bunkhouse and look over the plains toward the hamlet of Claybank, you may see or hear the pair of Long-billed Curlews that frequent the area. A walk to the south will take you through some badlands, both natural and artificial (from the old clay mines). Here you'll see or hear Say's Phoebe, Rock Wren, and Mountain Bluebird. The area may remind you of the Cypress Hills (page 93). It certainly reminded a Dusky Flycatcher of the same thing, as one spent the summer of 2014 in the ash woodlands on the slopes of the hills. These woodlands are a good place for Least Flycatcher, Clay-colored Sparrow, and Spotted Towhee.

GETTING THERE
From Regina, take Hwy. 6 south to the turnoff to Hwy. 334 at Corinne; from Moose Jaw, take Hwy. 1 to the Hwy. 39 exit, then go south on Hwy. 339 to Avonlea. (If you're coming from Moose Jaw, you should visit the birding sites in reverse order.) Your first stop will be (road conditions permitting) down a typical prairie road. At the junction of Hwy. 334 and Grid 623, turn south and bird along a 3.2 km (2 mi.) stretch of road, making a U-turn to return to Hwy. 334. Your next stop will be the Avonlea Badlands, which can be accessed on a trail on the left about 1 km past the sign on Hwy. 334 for Grid 623. Back on Hwy. 334, head west/left for 5.2 km to Avonlea. From Avonlea, take Hwy. 334 south and then east for 6.8 km to Dunnet Park. Upon returning to Hwy. 339 in Avonlea, turn left to head west for 8 km. If the road is passable, head west on the dirt road for 1.6 km

and then north for 3.2 km rather than taking the two speed curves on the highway. In either event, your next stop will be the Brick Plant, access for which is 6.4 km from the first speed curve.

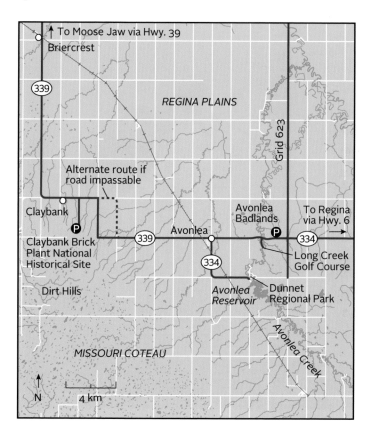

An adult Black-necked Stilt out for a walk with one of its four young.

ALAN R. SMITH

17

CHAPLIN LAKE

THIS AREA IS the largest covered in the Saskatchewan portion of this guide. It includes (from east to west) Chaplin, Reed, and "Francis" Lakes, all of which are easily accessed along or from the Trans-Canada Hwy. Chaplin Lake is a very large saline lake (6,450 ha/15,900 acres), which was in many dry years a lakebed, and in wetter years drained south into Chaplin Creek, then into the Wood River, and finally into Old Wives Lake. With the opening of a sodium sulphate mine in the town of Chaplin in 1948, the situation changed dramatically. Water was diverted from the Wood River, up Chaplin Creek, and into the north end of Chaplin Lake, which was divided into numerous basins. The basins were created to control the evaporation of water concentrating the sodium sulphate. The lake also supports a brine

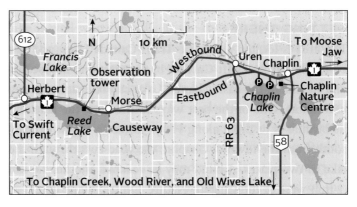

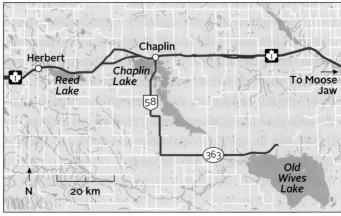

—18—

LEADER

T HE TOWN OF Leader lies just south of the South Saskatchewan River and the bridge of the same name. The area has the most extensive riparian woodlands along the entire South Saskatchewan River in Saskatchewan and the largest expanse of wooded country between the Cypress Hills and the aspen parkland. Most of the woodlands are composed of Plains Cottonwood. The lower reaches of the tributary creeks are covered in Manitoba Maple, while the upper reaches are clothed in Trembling Aspen. Large areas are covered in thickets of buffaloberry, rose, and other shrubs. Portions of the alluvial flats have been cleared for pivot irrigation.

With such a wide diversity of habitats, it's not surprising that there's an equally diverse flora and fauna. Large

The Leader area is perhaps the best place in the province to see a Red-headed Woodpecker. NICK SAUNDERS

numbers of Mule and White-tailed Deer inhabit the area.
The cutbanks along the river from the Leader Bridge to the
Alberta border are used for denning by one of only two populations of Prairie Rattlesnakes in Saskatchewan (the other
is in Grasslands National Park and vicinity).

One evening in late March 1997, a colleague and friend,
Don Weidl, and I were surveying for owls in the Estuary
area. When we weren't actually surveying, I had the radio
on. As we drove into the valley near the ferry, the radio fell
silent due to poor reception. Reception briefly returned with
the three words "Great Horned Owl"—and right at that
moment a Great Horned Owl flew across the road! Creepy,
but true!

BIRDING GUIDE
Since most of the land in this area is either privately owned
or Crown lease, public access to the river is somewhat limited. There are, however, enough areas where the river can
be reached to do some good birding. The road to Checkerboard Hill is good for Long-billed Curlew and other
grassland birds. A spectacular view of the South Saskatchewan River Valley awaits you at the Hill. Look up for raptors,
but also watch where you're walking, as this is the site of
most northerly hibernaculum of the Prairie Rattlesnake in
Saskatchewan. Driving west toward the ferry, you'll be on
a stretch of road that traverses a large stabilized sand dune
area, a good place to spot Sharp-tailed Grouse, Mourning
Dove, and Vesper Sparrow.

Once on the grid, follow it west and then north to
the ferry. The ferry runs to the north bank of the South

and adjacent uplands. After driving north for 6.4 km, turn west at the intersection and continue for another 9.0 km to the pull-in spot at Checkerboard Hill. Backtrack 2.6 km, then turn south for 6.4 km to get onto Grid 741 and drive 17.5 km west and north on Grid 635 to reach the ferry.

To reach the Sand Hills from Leader, drive 20 km (12 mi.) east on Hwy. 32 and turn south just past the village of Sceptre. This road (RR 243) travels through intensely farmed country before you reach the northwest corner of the Sand Hills. Drive south 10 km, taking the speed curve 1.6 km to the west (TWP Rd. 212) where you again turn south at the intersection (RR 244, unsignposted but obvious). After about 6 km you'll enter the Sand Hills. A further 2 km will take you to a turnoff where you can park and explore the active dunes.

N

8 km

To Kindersley and Hwy. 7

Grid 635

21

South Saskatchewan River

Grid 635

Estuary
Ferry

Leader Bridge

Red Deer R.

Twp. Rd. 232

Grid 635

Checkerboard
Hill

RR 272

RR 264

Grid 741

Leader

32

21

To Sceptre & the
Great Sand Hills

To Maple Creek

The Green Heron is a rare but increasing visitor to the wooded banks of streams and lakes in the province. ALAN R. SMITH

19

REGINA

EGINA (LATIN FOR "Queen": the town was named in honour of Queen Victoria) has been the capital of Saskatchewan since the province's creation in 1905. The city's major park, the Wascana Centre, comprises 930 ha (2,300 acres) of buildings, lawns, and trees surrounding Wascana Lake and Wascana Marsh, which were both formed by the damming of Wascana Creek and the subsequent deepening of the basin in 1931 and again in the winter of 2003–4 (the latter became known as the "Big Dig"). The park is larger than both New York City's Central Park and Vancouver's Stanley Park. The lake and marsh area includes several small islands: Willow, Spruce, Pine, Goose, and Tern Islands.

Because the surrounding plains are nearly devoid of trees and in many years bereft of standing water, the park and surrounding well-treed urban area act as a trap for migrating waterfowl and songbirds. Partly because of this richness and partly because of the large number of birders, Regina has the longest bird list of any equal-sized area in the province. It's therefore a great place to bird for any out-of-province birders who have only a few hours on their hands and want to make the most of being in Saskatchewan. Birding is best in the spring, but other seasons have their highlights.

Saskatchewan has only about 1.1 million people over an area almost the same size as Texas, which has 28 million souls. Of our population, I would say that fewer than 100 are active and knowledgeable birders. The chances of running into a fellow birder in Regina is, however, quite high. Birders of a feather flock together. A good place to commune with the friendly local birders is at the legislature for early spring gull-watching and at Goose Hill Park for warbler watching. I had a lifer "double header" while searching for a Red-bellied Woodpecker on November 2, 2001. I saw a Yellow-throated Warbler (Saskatchewan's second record) first and eventually saw the original species of interest. This is an example of Patagonia Picnic Table Effect, a phenomenon in which an influx of birders following the discovery of a rare bird at a location results in the discovery of further rarities at that location.

BIRDING GUIDE

Perhaps the best place to start an early morning bird walk is Wascana Park. In the winter, large but variable numbers of Canada Geese, a few Mallards, and occasional other waterfowl persist. Townsend's Solitaire are semiregular, especially in the cedars near the Royal Saskatchewan Museum. Varied Thrushes are less common and more liable to be seen at feeders in the older residential areas, such as the Lakeview district across from the legislature. Both Red and White-winged Crossbills are winter visitors, as "regular" as these species can be, in the towering spruce of the park. Merlins and increasingly Sharp-shinned Hawks may be seen hunting these and other wintering passerines. Otherwise rare in the province in the winter, both Red-tailed Hawk and American Crow often frequent the downtown core (perhaps because of its warm microclimate). A trip to the surrounding countryside should reveal a few Snowy Owls and, in early winter, Rough-legged Hawks.

In the early spring, the first main event is gull watching. This takes place on the ice of Wascana Lake off the legislature, and near the city landfill that includes the "snow dump" area at the corner of McDonald and Fleet Streets and ponds surrounding the landfill. Gulls feeding at the landfill typically roost on the ice of the lake until it melts, but they also frequent the snow dump and nearby wetlands. Most are Franklin's, Ring-billed, California, or Herring Gulls, but Thayer's and Glaucous Gulls are also regulars. Since 2005, Lesser Black-backed Gulls have also become regular. Rarities include Mew, Iceland, Slaty-backed, Western, Glaucous-winged, and Great Black-backed Gulls. Except for the Mew, most of the rarer gulls are much less frequent in the fall. Three km (1.9 mi.) north on Fleet St. will take you to the "Cement Plant Slough," the site of several rare gull records and, later in the season, some egret records.

As the spring thaw progresses, and the lake and marsh become live with migrant waterfowl and grebes, a few Clark's Grebe and Eurasian Wigeon and fair numbers of Greater Scaup have been seen. Later in the spring, successive waves of sparrows, thrushes, and finally flycatchers, vireos (including a few Yellow-throated), and warblers take the stage. Just about every species of warbler recorded in Saskatchewan has been seen in the park over the years. Common spring species include Ovenbird; Northern Waterthrush; and Mourning, Cape May, Blackburnian, Black-throated Green, and Canada Warblers, while rarities have included Northern Parula, and Golden-winged, Blue-winged, Prothonotary, Hooded, Black-throated Blue, Pine, Black-throated Gray, and Townsend's Warblers. All three tanager species should be looked for especially in the spring, the most common being Western, with a number of older Scarlet Tanager records, and five Summer Tanager records since the beginning of the 21st century.

Summer brings a few Green Herons, with sightings increasing along the shore of the lake and marsh, while overhead a few Chimney Swifts have been seen in and around Wascana Park on evenings in recent years. Wascana Marsh is the nesting ground for a wide variety of marsh birds, including Eared Grebe, Black Tern, Forster's Tern, Sora Rail, and Marsh Wren. Canada Geese are so ubiquitous as to be a nuisance. The Waterfowl Display Ponds on the south shore of the marsh are a great spot for Wood Duck.

Fall specialties on Wascana Lake and Marsh include Pacific Loon and Surf and Black Scoters. Most of the warblers mentioned for the spring are also seen in fall migration, although Black-throated Blue Warblers are more common in the fall than in spring. Several fall records of Red-bellied Woodpecker may foreshadow the first breeding of the species in the province; this is in contrast with declining records of Red-headed Woodpecker.

Three kilometres south of the interchange at Albert St. and Ring Rd. is a large wetland named after a defunct drive-in movie theatre. "Cinema Six Slough," as it's known, hosts large numbers and a wide variety of shorebirds, especially in the spring. Rarities have included Eurasian Wigeon, Harlequin Duck, Black-necked Stilt, Whimbrel, Buff-breasted Sandpiper, Sabine's Gull, and Smith's Longspur. Some impressive numbers of more common birds have included spring concentrations of 450 Black-bellied Plover, 7 Dunlin (a large number for the province!), and 27 Short-eared Owls.

If you're on your way to the south end of Last Mountain Lake, it's a good idea to stop at Condie Nature Refuge (just off Hwy. 11) as it's hosted a good variety of rarities, especially ducks, gulls, and terns, over the years. Bewick's race of the Tundra Swan has also been seen there in the fall.

GETTING THERE

Regina is accessible by road from Saskatoon on Hwy. 11 (258 km/160 mi. south), and from the rest of Canada by Hwy. 1, the Trans-Canada Hwy. It's also conveniently accessible by air from a number of major cities across North America. Condie Nature Refuge lies west of Hwy. 11—a 13.6 km drive northwest from the junction of Hwys. 11 and 6 on the northern outskirts of Regina. After driving 1.5 km on Hwy. 734, turn left (south) 300 m/yds to access the refuge.

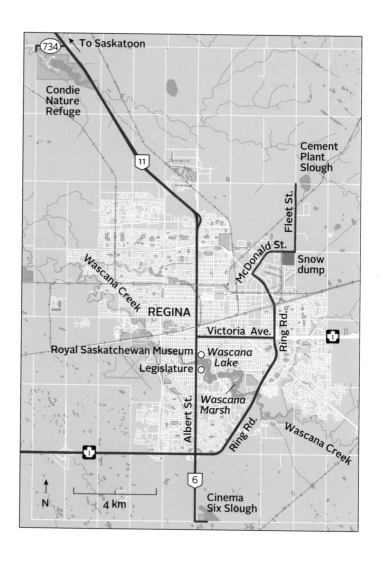

—20—
LAST MOUNTAIN
LAKE: SOUTH END

AST MOUNTAIN LAKE is a lake of two names: those living
at the south end know it as Long Lake, while those at
the north end correctly call it Last Mountain Lake. The
lake itself reflects this duality; the southern half is deep
with a narrow beach confined by a narrow valley, and at
Rowan's Ravine (which marks about the halfway point) the
lake and beach widen as the topography slopes more gradually away. Water levels on Last Mountain Lake are kept
artificially high to provide for better recreation on the lake
itself and to control downstream flooding.

Two main areas are described in this section: the Regina
Beach–Little Arm area on the southwest side of the lake,
and the Valeport Marshes at the south end. The two areas
are remarkably different. The first is dominated by the Little

An adult male Harlequin Duck is always a delight to see. NICK SAUNDERS

Arm (the drowned estuary of the Arm River) and resort communities of (from west to east) Kinookimaw, Regina Beach, Buena Vista, and Lumsden Beach; the second by an uninhabited marsh of 900 ha (2,200 acres) on the flood plain of the unnamed river draining Last Mountain Lake into the Qu'Appelle River. Both areas can be reached from the picturesque town of Lumsden.

Much of what we know of birds, and especially rarities, using the south end of the lake we owe to Bob Luterbach of Regina. Bob has diligently and patiently monitored the fall water bird migration in the Little Arm to Lumsden Beach area since the early 1980s. His efforts have transformed the status of Surf and Black Scoters, Long-tailed Duck, Barrow's Goldeneye, Pacific Loon, and Glaucous Gull from that of accidental to rare, to regular or nearly regular. He has also added or helped add records of such rarities as Slaty-backed Gull and Black-legged Kittiwake, and three of the four records of Ancient Murrelet. His efforts in spring, summer, and fall at the Valeport Marshes and adjacent Last Mountain Lake have been no less impressive, with over 55 records of Clark's Grebe. Bob has always unselfishly shared his observations with the birding community.

BIRDING GUIDE

The Regina Beach–Little Arm area is best visited in the fall, while the Valeport area is good from spring through the fall. When looking for rarities in the Regina Beach–Little Arm area (these occur mainly in the late fall), it's best to check all the areas from the Little Arm to Buena Vista, even Lumsden Beach. This is because birds move along the lakeshore and even across the lake to the resort communities on the other side. Check the waters at all access points for loons, including the rare Red-throated, Pacific, and Yellow-billed. Sea and bay ducks include the Greater Scaup, King and Common Eiders, Harlequin and Long-tailed Ducks, all three scoters, and Barrow's Goldeneye; all but the eiders and Harlequin Duck are regular or close to regular. Gulls have included Mew, Thayer's, Iceland, Lesser Black-backed, Slaty-backed, Glaucous-winged, Glaucous, Great Black-backed, and Sabine's, as well as Black-legged Kittiwake. Of these, only the Glaucous is regular, but one or more of the other species is recorded nearly every fall. Only eight records of four members of the auk family have been recorded for Saskatchewan, with six records from Regina Beach–Little Arm including single records of Black and Pigeon Guillemots, and four records of Ancient Murrelet (all of the latter in "Trestle Bay"). Other rare water birds have included Red Phalarope, and Pomarine and Parasitic Jaegers.

Upon reaching Regina Beach, continue straight ahead down McNabb Rd. past the hamlet of Kinookimaw and onto a trail that takes you to the point between Little Arm and "Trestle Bay." A railroad trestle formerly crossed the narrows, giving rise to this local name for that portion of the lake north of the point. Be careful driving the trail, as it is extremely rutted and should be navigated with great care, especially if you're in a passenger car. Returning to McNabb Rd., you can check out Kinookimaw, but this must be done on foot. Return to McNabb Rd. and drive to the junction with Hwy. 54. Turn left at the junction onto Centre St. and proceed through the town of Regina Beach and park at the foot of the wharf. Parking is good here, with great views of the lake and a beach used by roosting gulls. If you carry on to Lumsden Beach, you'll have to park up top and walk down the hill with your scope and tripod to the beach for an excellent wide-angle view of the lake.

On your way to Valeport Marsh, the towns of Lumsden and Craven are worth a walkabout; the former has yielded such rarities as White-winged Dove, Red-headed Woodpecker, Northern Cardinal, and Lazuli Bunting. The marsh can be accessed on both the south and north sides. To access the south side, turn left onto Whitmore Farm Rd. just before you cross the bridge as you approach Craven. On your left, the north-facing slope of the valley is well treed; listen for forest birds, including Black-billed Cuckoo and Veery. On your right is the marsh, where you should hear Sedge and Marsh Wrens, and LeConte's and Nelson's Sparrows. The north side of the marsh can be reached in three places. The first is 4 km (2.5 mi.) north of Craven. Here you can turn off to a small parking lot; you may have to be there early as fishermen have often taken all the spots. This site gives you access to a dike that crosses to the south side of the marsh. About 1 km farther down is a place to park with a good view overlooking much of the marsh—a good place to look for Great Egrets. The final spot is the picnic site, 700 m/yds along from the second parking spot. This is one of three areas (the others being the north end of Last Mountain Lake and Reed Lake) where Clark's Grebe has been found nesting in the province. Upward of 15 birds have been seen, and birds have been present from mid-April to late September. Keep a lookout for gulls and terns, including rare Caspian and Arctic Terns.

GETTING THERE

The Regina Beach and Valeport areas may be reached from Hwy. 11, which connects Regina and Saskatoon. If you're coming from Regina, Condie Nature Refuge (page 125), which is just off the highway, is worth a stop for water birds. To reach Regina Beach–Little Arm, take Hwy. 54 north from Hwy. 11, an intersection that is 6 km (4 mi.) west of Lumsden and 8 km east of Disley; after 13 km, the road turns northwest at Buena Vista. After 3.7 km, you'll reach the junction of McNabb Rd. (head west for Kinookimaw) and Centre St. (head north for the Regina Beach Wharf). For the Buena Vista access, return to the junction and take Hwy. 54 east for 4 km. The shoreline in Buena Vista is best accessed off Lakeview Cres. After returning to Hwy. 54, drive 1.6 km south to Chown St. Drive 2.7 km down Chown St. to Lumsden Beach. To reach Valeport Marsh, take Hwy. 20 northeast 7 km from the town of Lumsden toward Craven, and turn left at Whitmore Farm Rd. For the north side of the marsh, drive northwest from Craven; there are three parking spots starting from 4 km northwest of Craven.

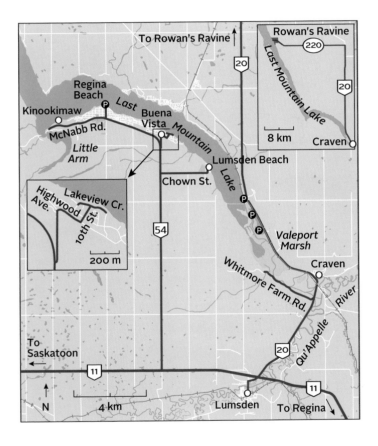

Forster's Tern is the white tern most likely to be seen in marshy areas.
ALAN R. SMITH

21

LAST MOUNTAIN LAKE: NORTH END

AST MOUNTAIN LAKE National Wildlife Area, located at the north end of Last Mountain Lake (known informally as Long Lake), is home to the oldest bird sanctuary in North America (established 1887). As its informal name suggests, Last Mountain Lake is a long one: 93 km (58 mi.). The National Wildlife Area includes the northern end of the lake, which is characterized by several shallow bays or "fingers," portions of which have been dammed, forming several basins. The Wildlife Area includes some 15,602 ha (38,553 acres) of lake, marsh, and upland at the north end of the lake. About 54% of the total area is in native grasslands, and initiatives are underway to restore more areas. Controlled fires and grazing are used to

In the fall, numbers and the variety of migrants are greater and the migratory period is longer. A good time of year is mid-August, when the variety of warblers is at its greatest. A dozen species can easily be seen in a day, and the odds are better than even that you'll see a Canada Warbler during this period. Late September is also good—the hedgerows teem with many species of sparrow, Palm Warbler, and the occasional Winter Wren. A Sharp-shinned Hawk is almost always seen hunting along the hedgerows. Upward of 100 Hooded Mergansers can be seen offshore at this time of year.

Next it's time to tour the National Wildlife Area. Go back to the park access road, and turn north at the deserted farmstead. On the way, keep a close eye on the hedgerows for Loggerhead Shrike; in the fall the fields should be alive with Sandhill Cranes and geese. This stretch of road is the site of the province's first and only record of Northern Wheatear. After 10 km (6.2 mi.), turn west at the T-junction. After about 2 km, you'll pass Lanigan Creek and the marshes of the north end. When the water levels are good, it's a great place to observe summer resident and migrant shorebirds. Forster's Tern can often be seen sitting on partially submerged fence posts. Great, Snowy, and Cattle Egrets, Little Blue Heron, and White-faced Ibis have all been observed here and at the Lanigan Creek Dam. The picnic area here is a good place to see raptors, and in the fall, large mixed flocks of swallows. At 3.2 km from the T-junction, turn south/ left, continue for 600 m/yds, and then stop at the parking lot just past the access to the boardwalk and a floating bird blind. The marshes here are a good site to hear the much sought-after Yellow Rail (as well as the other two rails), LeConte's and Nelson's Sparrows, and Sedge and Marsh Wrens. The Wetland Nature Trail follows a loop where you can walk toward the picnic site and back to the dike.

Returning to the parking lot, drive south and turn left and stop at the dead end near the rock pile; you'll have to walk the rest of the way to the dam on Lanigan Creek, but it's usually well worth it. Avian fishers are almost always here, and include American White Pelican, Double-crested Cormorant, and Black-crowned Night-Heron. A colony of Cliff Swallows nests under the dam. Return to the road and drive 350 m/yds, at which point you'll come to a fork in the road. Baseball great Yogi Berra once said, "When you come to a fork in the road, take it." Follow his advice here. If you go left, it takes you to the observation tower. If you're here in the late fall, you'll see huge flocks of Snow Geese and other waterfowl. The best time to arrive is midday, as most birds are out feeding in distant fields in the mornings and evenings. If you take the fork to the right, it takes you to the Grassland Nature Trail, which, as its name suggests, is a good place to see some of the grassland birds. You have a better than even chance of seeing Smith's Longspur here (or near the Wetland Nature Trail) in late September. They are, however, annoyingly secretive, often flushing before you can get a good look at them on the ground, but look for extensive white in the tail in flight. Sadly, another longspur— the Chestnut-collared—is no longer found here or anywhere in the Wildlife Area, as they've retreated southward past Regina; Sprague's Pipits and Baird's Sparrows are, however, easily found in season. Until the flood that occurred around

2010, you could continue to drive across two "fingers" north to the headquarters of the NWA. Unfortunately, as of time of writing, you'll have to return whence you came.

After returning to the gate, head to the headquarters of the Wildlife Area. In the fall, watch for Whooping Cranes feeding in the fields along the stretch of road leading south to the headquarters. Next, drive south from the junction at the headquarters. The road takes you back to the "Fingers"—a great place to see American White Pelican, night-heron and Common Tern, and in the fall, huge rafts of American Coot and kleptoparasitic American Wigeon. Poor divers—the wigeon take advantage of the food that the coots bring up from the bottom.

Northern Harriers are always in evidence over the prairies and marshes of the Wildlife Area. Keep your eyes peeled for the Short-eared Owl, for this is the best place in Saskatchewan to consistently see this now rare species. In the spring, the fallow fields to the north and west of the Wildlife Area are a good place to check for foraging shorebirds. Large numbers of Black-bellied Plover and American Golden-Plover and lesser numbers of Ruddy Turnstone, Red Knot, and Buff-breasted Sandpiper may be seen feeding in these fields. The exact location of these fallow fields varies from year to year, depending on crop rotations. On May 21, 1972, artist and conservationist Fred Lahrman saw a mixed flock of 5,000 turnstones and knots in one such field. It must have been quite a sight!

GETTING THERE

Last Mountain Regional Park and the National Wildlife Area may be reached from Saskatoon by travelling 125 km

The Glaucous Gull is a rare but regular spring and fall visitor to southern
Saskatchewan, especially the Saskatoon and Regina areas. NICK SAUNDERS

(78 mi.) east on Hwy. 16 to Lanigan, then south on Hwy. 20 to the Last Mountain Regional Park access road (16 km south of Nokomis). From Regina, take Hwy. 11 north for 22 km to Lumsden, then drive north on Hwy. 20 to the park access road (5.5 km north of Govan). To reach the National Wildlife Area from the park, drive 5 km east from the park gate, turn north at the crossroads by a deserted farmstead with spruce trees, and then drive north for 10 km until you reach a T-junction. Turn west/left and drive 3.2 km to pass through the gate on your left, which will take you to the boardwalk, floating blind, and Wetland Trail (600 m/yds); access to Lanigan Creek Dam (3.8 km); access to the observation tower (4.3 km); and the "Fingers" and the Grasslands Trail (6 km). Return to the gate, turn left, drive 3.3 km, and turn left again to drive south for 3.2 km to the headquarters of the Wildlife Area. Another 2 km farther south takes you to back to the "Fingers."

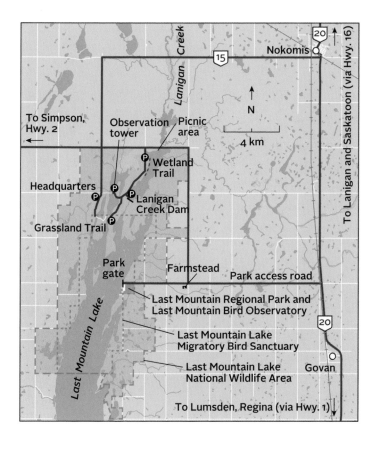

To Simpson, Hwy. 2

N

4 km

Lanigan Creek

Nokomis

To Lanigan and Saskatoon (via Hwy. 16)

Observation tower

Picnic area

Wetland Trail

Headquarters

Lanigan Creek Dam

Grassland Trail

Park gate

Farmstead

Park access road

Last Mountain Regional Park and Last Mountain Bird Observatory

Last Mountain Lake Migratory Bird Sanctuary

Last Mountain Lake National Wildlife Area

Last Mountain Lake

Govan

To Lumsden, Regina (via Hwy. 1)

American White Pelicans are often seen fishing below "the weir."

ALAN R. SMITH

22

SASKATOON

OCATED ON THE banks of the South Saskatchewan River, the city of Saskatoon is the northern rival for Regina in everything—including birds. The city is named after a local species of a Juneberry of the same name, which in turn is derived from the Cree word *misâskwatômina*. From an ornithological point of view, one of the city's main claims to fame is its Merlin population. While it may not be the world's largest, it's definitely the best known, having been the subject of intense study for over 20 years. Saskatoon takes second place after Regina for the total number of species of birds recorded, but almost always bests Regina for the number of species recorded on the Christmas Bird Count. Birding in Saskatoon is good in spring, summer, and fall; and, for the prairies, even in the winter.

I grew up in Saskatoon in the 1950s and 1960s. In the early 1960s, my mother saw my growing interest in birds and encouraged me to join the Saskatoon Natural History Society. I was fortunate enough to have a number of mentors from the society. From Frank Roy, I learned to appreciate the beauty of birds in plumage and in song, from Dr. Stuart Houston I learned the importance of bird banding to the study of birds, from Dr. Bernie Gollop I learned how important it was to carefully document bird migration, and from Jim Slimmon I learned how to find and respectfully monitor bird nests. This group was all about ornithology. Listing was important, but it was always done in the context of science—what birds, where, when, and in what habitats.

BIRDING GUIDE

Many of the best birding areas in Saskatoon are located near or along the South Saskatchewan River. These are mapped from north to south, first on the west side of the river and then on the east side. The western sites are all along or just off Spadina Cres., which follows the river. The weir (at 33rd St.) south on the west side of the river to University Bridge (25th St.) is almost always good. The water just below the weir is a favourite feeding spot for summering American White Pelican, and (especially in the fall) for various diving ducks, including the occasional Greater Scaup, Harlequin Duck, Long-tailed Duck, and Barrow's Goldeneye. The island above the weir hosts a colony of breeding Ring-billed and California Gulls, as well as many nesting Canada Geese. The woods south of the weir are a good spot for spring and fall migrant songbirds. The American Dipper has twice been seen in fall below the weir. During the winter, the river from well below the weir all the way to the Queen Elizabeth Power Station hosts hundreds of Common Goldeneye and usually a few Common Merganser; at night, most wintering waterfowl roost near the Bessborough Hotel farther south on Spadina.

Your next site is Holiday Park, which can be accessed off Spadina on Schuyler St. It was the former site of a sanatorium, and it has attracted several rarities. The first of these was a Golden-crowned Sparrow, which was seen by one of my mentors, Frank Roy, and yours truly on May 18, 1963. I was a 14-year-old boy at the time—and from then on I was hooked on birding! Other, more recent, rarities have included Northern Cardinal, Pine Warbler, and Cassin's Finch. Summer residents include Least Flycatcher, Warbling and Red-eyed Vireos, Gray Catbird, and Brown Thrasher. One of the best places to observe gulls is along the river near the Queen Elizabeth Power Station, a couple of kilometres south on Spadina. You can park in an unpaved lot near the river just north of the power station and watch gulls moving between the nearby landfill and sandbars on the river. Gull watching is best in April and October. Most are common species—Franklin's, Ring-billed, California, and Herring—but a few are Thayer's, Iceland, Lesser Black-backed, or Glaucous Gulls, and a Slaty-backed Gull was seen in the spring of 2009.

On the east side of the river, and at some distance from it, are two sites well worth visiting. The first is the Forestry Farm Park. Originally established as a tree nursery to supply the farming community with shelterbelts, the area has been transformed into a zoo and multi-purpose recreational site. It can be reached from Attridge Dr., east off Circle Dr. Because of the planting of fruiting trees and conifers, this park is good for Townsend's Solitaire and crossbills in the winter, and many different migrants in the spring and fall.

The second is President Murray Park, named in honour of Walter Charles Murray, first president of the University of Saskatchewan. The park is a 3 ha (7 acre) tract between Wiggins Ave. and McKinnon Ave. and Aird St. and Colony St. The main arteries are Clarence Ave., which is one block to the west, and College Dr., which is four blocks to the north; both converge on 25th St. (University Bridge). The outstanding feature of the park is its 500 mature White Spruce, which attract a good variety of birds. Merlin, Black-billed Magpie, Blue Jay, and Red-breasted Nuthatch are year-round residents. In the fall, the site is often used as a roost by upward of 3,000 Common Crow. During the late spring and early fall, it's particularly attractive to Olive-sided and Yellow-bellied Flycatchers and spruce-loving migrant warblers, such as Cape May, Black-throated Green, and Bay-breasted. During the winter it's a great place to see boreal forest birds such as Black-backed and American Three-toed Woodpeckers, Boreal Chickadee, Golden-crowned Kinglet, and both species of crossbills.

Hot spots along the east bank of the river are Cosmopolitan and Diefenbaker Parks. Located between the Broadway and 25th St. bridges and backed by Saskatchewan Cres., Cosmopolitan Park includes one of the few natural stretches of riverbank in the city. The northern portion of the park is a good place to observe woodland birds, especially migrant thrushes, warblers, and sparrows. Farther down Saskatchewan Cres., then west briefly on Taylor St. and south on St. Henry Ave., is Diefenbaker Park. With its panoramic view, the park is good for watching birds on the river and sandbars, and for raptors migrating up or down the river valley.

Two other good spots are the Hudson Bay Slough near the airport and the campus of the University of Saskatchewan.

GETTING THERE

Saskatoon can be accessed by road from Regina by travelling north on Hwy. 11 for 259 km (161 mi.), and from the rest of Canada by Hwy. 16, the Yellowhead Highway. It can also be easily accessed by air from major cities across North America.

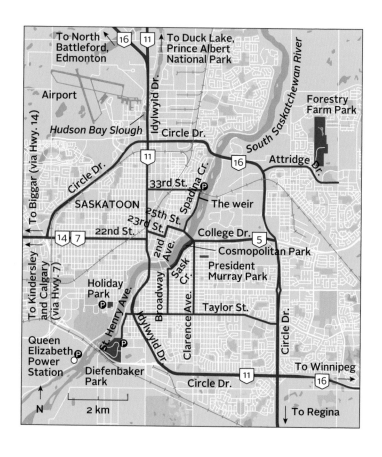

To North Battleford, Edmonton

To Duck Lake, Prince Albert National Park

Airport

South Saskatchewan River

Forestry Farm Park

Hudson Bay Slough

Circle Dr.

Idylwyld Dr.

To Biggar (via Hwy. 14)

Circle Dr.

33rd St.

Spadina Cr.

Attridge Dr.

SASKATOON

25th St.

The weir

23rd St.

22nd St.

2nd Ave.

College Dr.

Cosmopolitan Park

To Kindersley and Calgary (via Hwy. 7)

Holiday Park

President Murray Park

Broadway

Sask Cr.

Clarence Ave.

Taylor St.

St. Henry Ave.

Queen Elizabeth Power Station

Idylwyld Dr.

Circle Dr.

To Winnipeg

Diefenbaker Park

Circle Dr.

N   2 km

To Regina

23

DUCK LAKE–
MACDOWALL

TRAVELLERS ON HWY. 11 between Saskatoon and Prince Albert will notice that the highway takes them through a pine, aspen, and spruce forest between the town of Duck Lake and the village of Macdowall. This area and other nearby tracts of forest are officially known as Nisbet Provincial Forest, the core of this birding area. Provincial forests are Crown lands managed by the province not only for forestry purposes, but also for livestock grazing, hunting, trapping, and recreation.

The Duck Lake–Macdowall area has a long history of ornithological exploration. The first of many distinguished naturalists and scientists to study its rich and varied wildlife were Sir John Richardson and Thomas Drummond, who

It is unfortunate that the brilliant ruby crown of the male Ruby-crowned Kinglet is rarely seen. NICK SAUNDERS

served under British explorer Sir John Franklin. Richardson first visited the area with the first Franklin expedition in 1820. He spent most of May at Fort Carlton, which lies just southwest of the Nisbet Forest, and made a subsequent visit in the spring of 1827. He described several species new to science, including the Gray-crowned Rosy-Finch, Clay-colored Sparrow, and Smith's Longspur. Next came naturalist Thomas Blakiston, who served in an expedition led by Captain John Palliser. Blakiston studied the wildlife of the region from October 1857 to June 1858. In the early part of the 20th century, several natural history museums sent expeditions to the area to collect bird specimens. The most famous of these museum men was author Farley Mowat, who spent part of the summer of 1939 near Fort Carlton.

On December 20, 2001, a colleague named Keith Hobson and I were conducting a Christmas Bird Count in the Nisbet Forest. In a nearby bog we saw a Northern Shrike perched atop a spruce a few hundred metres away. Suddenly, the shrike flew toward us, landing in a tall shrub only metres distant. It then flew down from its perch, retrieved a small mammal hidden beneath the snow, and flew off with it. It seemed to us that the shrike—bold, fast, and direct—didn't want us to get its food!

BIRDING GUIDE

The rich birdlife of the Nisbet Forest area has been documented for 200 years, a period that has seen great changes. When Richardson and Drummond were there, grassland birds, such as the Ferruginous Hawk, were common. The species was still common in Mowat's day. Today, with the suppression of wildfires, grassland birds are no longer common. They've been replaced by mixed-wood forest birds, which are otherwise found 100 km (62 mi.) farther north at Emma Lake. This area is an excellent one for birders wishing to make a day trip from Saskatoon. The best time to visit this area is June, when the singing of boreal forest birds is at its peak.

Perhaps the best place to bird is along Eb's Cross-country Ski Trails, north of Duck Lake. Park at the trails' north parking lot, and take the Beaverlodge Loop, where you'll encounter most of the varied habitats in the Nisbet Forest. The routes are well signed. If you go in winter, walk on the side of the trail so you don't ruin the ski tracks.

In summer, Hermit Thrush and Blue-headed Vireo are fairly common and Brown Creeper and Connecticut Warbler occasional in the Jack Pine of the first kilometre of the loop. In the White Spruce and Trembling Aspen forests between Willow and Beaverlodge sloughs you should see or hear spruce-loving warblers, including Cape May and Black-throated Green Warblers in the canopy, Nashville and Chestnut-sided Warblers in the understory, and the odd Winter Wren in the deadfalls. American Redstart and Rose-breasted Grosbeak are common in the tall Balsam Poplars along Beaverlodge Slough. Marsh birds such as the Wilson's Snipe and Black Tern are frequent over the slough, and Yellow Rail has been recorded on at least two occasions. Evening Grosbeaks are often heard overhead, while Broad-winged Hawks wait patiently for prey. It's best to retrace your steps back to the parking lot, as it may be difficult, and not even necessary, to follow the rest of the loop. Gray

Jay, and Boreal and Black-capped Chickadees are present year-round, and in winter these woods are a great place to observe Hairy, Downy, American Three-toed, Black-backed, and Pileated Woodpeckers.

Just before Macdowall, take the road to the left (it's not signposted), cross the railroad tracks, pass one road and turn at the second, and continue to follow the road as it traverses the Nisbet Forest in a southwesterly direction. This is usually a quiet road, and it's a good place to listen for calling owls (Great Horned, Barred, and Northern Saw-whet) and drumming woodpeckers, and later in the spring, songbirds. This road eventually connects with Grid 783, which returns you to the town of Duck Lake. Back in town, you can take a short drive along the east shore of Duck Lake. No one knows much about the bird use of the lake, but Virginia Rail has been heard there. If you have time, a trip to Fort Carlton is well worth the time. Birds here are more typical of the aspen parkland biome south of the Nisbet Forest, and include Swainson's Hawk, American Avocet, Cedar Waxwing, Spotted Towhee, and Clay-colored Sparrow.

Not far from the town of Duck Lake is Batoche National Historic Site, the location of the historic Battle of Batoche during the Northwest Rebellion of 1885. The battle resulted in the defeat of Louis Riel and his Métis forces by Major General Frederick Middleton and the North West Field Force.

GETTING THERE

To reach Duck Lake from Saskatoon, take Hwy. 11 north for 86 km (53 mi.); from Prince Albert, take Hwy. 1 south for 55 km. Eb's Cross-country Ski Trails are located on the west side of Hwy. 11, 19 km north of Duck Lake. Hwy. 212, west of Duck Lake, takes you directly to Fort Carlton (25 km one-way trip). Batoche can be reached by driving east on Hwy. 312 from Rosthern (a large town 21 km south of Duck Lake on Hwy. 11), just beyond the South Saskatchewan River, and turning north on Hwy. 225 for 10 km.

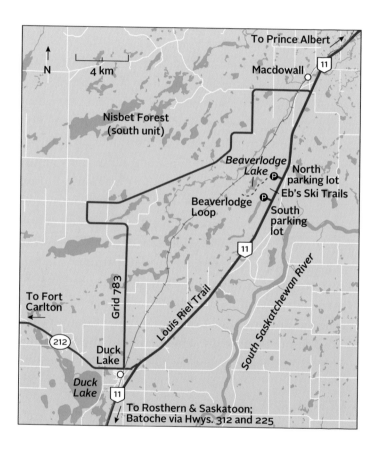

24

PRINCE ALBERT NATIONAL PARK

P RINCE ALBERT NATIONAL Park comprises 387,500 ha (957,500 acres) on the southern edge of the boreal forest. The northern part of the park is dominated by evergreens, giving way to mixed woods, and finally to aspen parkland and fescue grassland along the southern edge of the park. In contrast to the park's surroundings, which are agricultural on the southern boundary and subject to logging to the west, north, and east, much of the forest in the park is old growth. A recently proposed fire-management strategy would enhance biodiversity by allowing controlled burning, which would increase the diversity of stand ages throughout the park. The strategy would also reduce the potential for destructive fires due to the buildup of fuel in the form of dead and dying trees.

Male Blackburnian Warbler is inadvertently but aptly named for it has a lot of black and its head burns deep orange-red. NICK SAUNDERS

As is typical of the boreal forest, Prince Albert National Park is blessed with great natural diversity, a diversity that is enhanced by the absence of hunting and trapping. This is evident in the abundance of big game and fur-bearing mammals in comparison to the surrounding areas. Moose, Wapiti (Elk), and White-tailed Deer are found throughout the park. Woodland Caribou are found in the remote north, while Saskatchewan's only free-ranging herd of bison is found in the south. River Otter are easily observed in the park, especially at spring breakup. Observers can entertain realistic hopes of seeing Wolves, marten, and Fisher in this wildlife haven.

Back in 1980, in the days when I had a lot of spare time, I made a map superimposing all the breeding range maps in Godfrey's *Birds of Canada* on a single map to see which part of the country had the most breeding species. I won't go into great detail as to exactly how I did it, but basically I divided the country into small ecologically similar units. If the ranges consistently indicated that subdivision was warranted, I further subdivided these units. The result was surprising. The areas with the most breeding species, 170–180, were on the southern fringes of the boreal forest in western Canada from Edmonton through central Saskatchewan and the Manitoba Interlake to Winnipeg—higher than anywhere else in Canada and, according to two references that I had consulted, north of Mexico! In a way it's really not all that surprising. As well as having a great variety of forest birds—owls, woodpeckers, flycatchers, vireos, thrushes, sparrows, finches, and most importantly warblers—these areas have an unrivalled diversity of grebes and ducks.

BIRDING GUIDE

In the early spring, Waskesiu Lake and its surrounding area are an unparalleled place to listen for owls. Six species nest in the woodlands of the park and adjacent areas and may be heard in many areas, particularly on warm calm nights. For those interested in the Boreal Owl, it's vocal for an extremely short period from late March until early April; the other species call much later into the season. The best strategy is to drive along the roads and just listen. Good areas for Boreal Owls include the west end of McPhee Lake (which is just outside the park on Hwy. 264), and Hwy. 263, south of Waskesiu Lake.

A birding must is the Boundary Bog Nature Trail, which, as its name suggests, is about 1.5 km (just under 1 mi.) inside the eastern park boundary. A 2 km boardwalk allows you a "high and a dry" entry to the world of a Black Spruce bog. Here, permanent residents such as Ruffed and Spruce Grouse, Boreal Chickadee, and White-winged Crossbill are joined in summer by Olive-sided and Yellow-bellied Flycatchers, Philadelphia Vireo, Golden-crowned and Ruby-crowned Kinglets, Nashville and Palm Warblers (the former at its western limits), Lincoln's and Swamp Sparrows, and Rusty Blackbird.

Two roads lead west out of Waskesiu townsite to nearly encircle Waskesiu Lake. The Narrows Rd. leads to the First Narrows in the west end of the lake. Watch for Caspian Terns on the lake as you go. At the end of the road is the Treebeard Nature Trail, which runs for 1.2 km (0.7 mi.) through a stand of old-growth forest. The trail starts in Balsam Fir then moves into a White Spruce forest that hasn't burned since 1823. Now toppled giants, these trees are the product of nutrient-rich creeks tumbling out of the Waske-siu Hills. Here, summer-resident Blue-headed Vireo, Winter Wren, Swainson's Thrush, Bay-breasted, Blackburnian, and Black-throated Green Warblers, and Western Tanager join winter-resident Black-backed and Pileated Woodpeckers, Red-breasted Nuthatch, and Evening Grosbeak.

The other road, Kingsmere Rd., follows the north side of the lake. Directly opposite the Treebeard Trail is the Narrows Peninsula Trail. The forest here is much younger and is a good place for Hermit Thrush, and Tennessee, Mourning, and Chestnut-sided Warblers.

At the end of Kingsmere Rd. is the Kingsmere River, which drains Kingsmere Lake. A trail along the east side of the lake leads to the cabin and gravesite of Archibald Belaney—aka Great Gray Owl—on Ajawaan Lake. Just off the west side of Kingsmere, and connected to it by a narrow channel, is Bagwa Lake, the site of a 2014 Trumpeter Swan nesting.

The southern portion of the park along the Cookson Rd. (Grid 240) is also worth a visit. Because the habitat comprises semi-open stands of aspen, one can expect some different species—for example, Mourning Dove, Connecticut Warbler, Vesper Sparrow, and Baltimore Oriole. The range of the Eastern Whip-poor-will reaches its westernmost extent in this area.

Fall in the boreal forest is not as dramatic as on the prairies, as many species overfly the forest. But there are some highlights: hundreds of Common Loons and Red-necked Grebes may be seen on Kingsmere Lake and remote Crean

Lake, and rare ducks, including the Harlequin Duck and Barrow's Goldeneye, have been observed on Waskesiu Lake. Due to the lack of open country, large numbers of Horned Lark, American Pipit, and Lapland Longspur may be seen concentrated along roadsides in the late fall. Check all long-spurs for the odd Smith's Longspur.

GETTING THERE

Two routes take you to the Village of Waskesiu Lake, at the heart of the park. If you're in a hurry, take Hwy. 2 north for 75 km (47 mi.) from Prince Albert or south for 165 km from La Ronge, and then head west for 14 km on Hwy. 264, which is the main access to the park. If you're in no rush, I recommend the old road (Hwy. 263). To access it, take the Tweedsmuir exit west off Hwy. 2, 37 km north of Prince Albert. The Cookson Rd. (Grid 240) branches off Hwy. 263 near the southeastern entrance to the park and heads west along the southern edge of the park. The Boundary Bog Nature Trail is located 5.5 km east of the Waskesiu townsite. Two roads lead west out of Waskesiu townsite: the Narrows Rd. starts about 5 km south of town and west off the Lakeview Dr., while Kingsmere Rd. follows the north side of the lake.

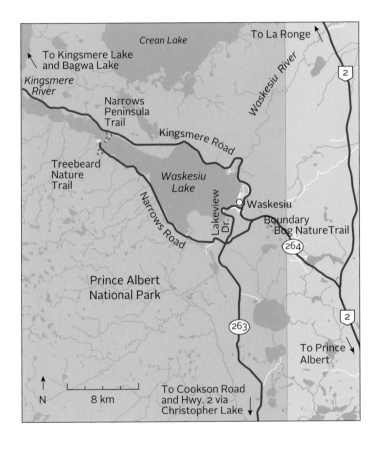

Crean Lake

To La Ronge

To Kingsmere Lake
and Bagwa Lake

Waskesiu River

Kingsmere
River

2

Narrows
Peninsula
Trail

Kingsmere Road

Treebeard
Nature
Trail

Waskesiu
Lake

Narrows Road

Lakeview Dr.

Waskesiu

Boundary
Bog NatureTrail

264

Prince Albert
National Park

263

2

To Prince
Albert

N

8 km

To Cookson Road
and Hwy. 2 via
Christopher Lake

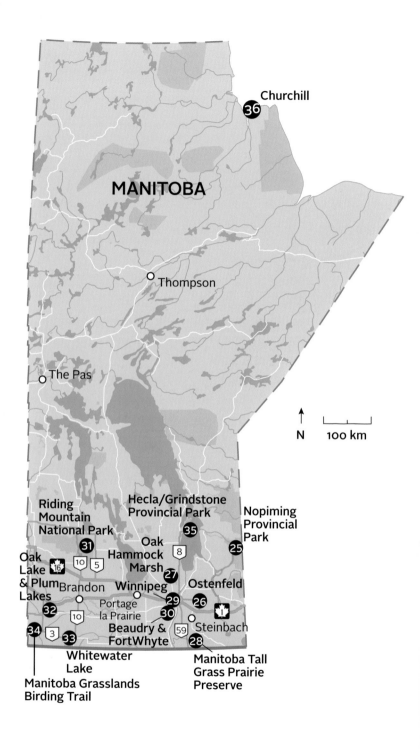

Churchill 36

MANITOBA

○ Thompson

○ The Pas

↑ N   ⊢————⊣ 100 km

Hecla/Grindstone
Provincial Park

Nopiming
Provincial
Park

Riding
Mountain
National Park   35

                    31   Oak
Oak   10   5   Hammock   8
Lake   16   Marsh
& Plum   Brandon   Winnipeg   25
Lakes   ○   Portage   27   Ostenfeld
          32   la Prairie   29   26
                              30   1
         34   3   Beaudry &   59 Steinbach
               33   FortWhyte ○
                              28

Whitewater
Lake   Manitoba Tall
                        Grass Prairie
Manitoba Grasslands   Preserve
Birding Trail

MANITOBA

NICOLA KOPER

The Northern Hawk Owl hunts during the day, unlike most owls.

PAULSON DES BRISAY

25

NOPIMING PROVINCIAL PARK

NOPIMING PROTECTS A beautiful fringe of the Canadian Shield where its granite rocks emerge east of Manitoba's tall-grass prairie ecoregion, and thus it's appropriately named after the Anishinabe word *noopiming*, meaning "entrance to the wilderness." It's much less well known and less populated than Whiteshell Provincial Park immediately to its south, which allows for a somewhat more wild-and-remote-feeling experience, although birders still enjoy the benefits of road access to a number of promising birding locations in a wide variety of different boreal habitats. Nopiming is also adjacent to Atikaki Provincial Park, to its north, and Woodland Caribou Provincial Park, to its east in Ontario. It's just one component of a massive interprovincial protected area providing protection to Woodland Caribou, Canada Lynx, Bobcat, and a wide variety of migratory and resident birds.

The southwest corner, just east of the junction between PR 314 and 315, is a relatively tall mixed-wood boreal forest with abundant arboreal lichen. As a result, south Nopiming is a hot spot in the province for Northern Parulas, with particularly high densities of this warbler around Bird Lake. The habitat becomes rockier and more Jack Pine dominated as you go east toward Davidson Lake, and boggier and more Black Spruce dominated as you travel north along PR 314. This provides a nice variety of avian communities over fairly small distances.

BIRDING GUIDE

My favourite way to bird in Nopiming is by canoe or kayak. This allows for relaxing observations of Common Loons (which I find unusually lovely when in their non-breeding plumage in October), Common Goldeneyes, Common and Hooded Mergansers, and other species that occupy open water during the breeding season. Lakesides are predominantly rocky in this region, with small extents of beach and bulrush-dominated wetland in some shallower areas, resulting in a few pairs of Solitary and Spotted Sandpipers, Red-winged Blackbirds, and Common Yellowthroats, and fairly abundant populations of Swamp Sparrows. However, canoe or kayak is also my favourite mode of transportation for observing forest-dwelling songbirds, as the lakesides provide close access to uplands that are uninhabited and inaccessible by road. In addition to species you would expect to find near water, such as Northern Waterthrush, I've had great observations of Bay-breasted and Black-throated Green Warblers from the water. While Nopiming is home to several canoe or kayak routes, simply putting a canoe in the water in one of the lakes off PR 314 or 315 will give plenty of opportunities for relaxing day-trip birding. Canoes can be rented from Nopiming Lodge on Bird Lake if you don't have one with you (call for availability: 204-884-2281).

Roadside birding and a few short hiking trails in Nopiming are also rewarding. When driving, stop at wetland-forest interfaces to listen for wetland species such as Alder Flycatchers and, if you're lucky, Yellow-bellied Flycatchers. This provides an opportunity to listen for forest songbirds as well. Nopiming has relatively few hiking trails, although a few unmarked trails add quality and quantity to the list. For birding, I would initially stick to the PR 315/Bird Lake Rd. corridor, although you may eventually want to take a trip up PR 314 for a boggier, more northern boreal environment. Good starting points for hikes are the trails around Tulabi campground. Don't overlook the short but pretty trail from the waterfall south to the public beach. The more heavily used, although unsigned, trails to the lookout and along the southeast side of Tulabi Lake (with some scrambling you can connect these as a loop), up to but also past the jumping rock, offer lovely views and are favoured by warblers, Winter Wrens, and Cedar Waxwings, among others. Another unsigned, underappreciated, and easily overlooked trail runs opposite the Flanders Lake cottages. It passes through Jack Pine and mixed-wood boreal and alongside a beaver pond, and ends at a Black Spruce swamp. Other trails can be found at the end of Flanders Lake Rd. and where PR 315 ends at the Ontario border just past the Davidson Lake boat launch, but watch for the occasional ATV.

Nopiming is on a busy migration flyway in the spring and fall. Early fall is the best time to catch Red-necked Grebes and the odd Pied-billed Grebe on the lakes, and Common Nighthawks on the wing. If you're lucky, you might find a Boreal Chickadee moving through. Winter birding is relatively sparse, although there are opportunities to observe Black-backed and Pileated Woodpeckers, over-wintering Great Gray Owls, and of course, the ever-present Ruffed Grouse. The area is heavily used by snowmobilers in winter, which significantly detracts from birding opportunities then.

GETTING THERE

It takes about two hours to drive to the edge of Nopiming Provincial Park from Winnipeg. Take Hwy. 59 to Libau, and go east/right on PR 317 to Lac du Bonnet for 46 km (29 mi.). Jog north on Hwy. 11 for just under 3 km, then go east on PR 313 until the junction with PR 315, where you turn left/north. The junction between PR 314 and 315 (now also called Bird Lake Rd.) is just past the sign indicating that you've entered the park. Most of the locations mentioned above are east (turn right at the PR 314/315 junction) along PR 315; the junction to the Bird Lake sites is 16.5 km east of the PR 314/315 junction, while the Ontario border, which intersects Davidson Lake, is another 12 km farther. If you go north on PR 314 from the junction with 315, most birding or lakeside opportunities are at least 28 km farther along the gravel road.

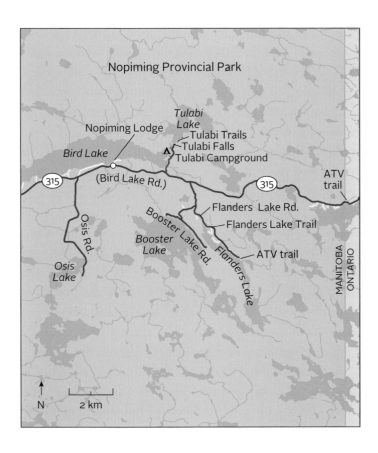

To get to the Tulabi campground trails, turn right onto PR 315 (also signed as Bird Lake Rd.) after the park entrance sign (at the PR 314/315 junction), and drive for 16.5 km (10.2 mi.). Tulabi campground is well signed, and is about five minutes' drive past the last of the Bird Lake cottage blocks. If the campground is open, drive to the main parking lot (closest to the waterfall). Follow the signs to Tulabi Falls and check out the short trail running along the southeast edge of the falls toward the campground (if you're standing on the deck over the falls, facing the parking lot, turn right). Then return to the parking lot and explore the trails around Tulabi Lake. To go to the rock lookout, take the unmarked trail that leads directly from the east side of the parking lot, before (and if you're facing Tulabi Lake, to the right of) the gate preventing vehicles from driving down to the lake. If you go past the lookout after enjoying the view, look for a trail that with some scrambling and good-quality hiking boots will bring you to the lake, where you can return to the parking lot along a narrow trail running close to the shore. Alternatively, walk to the small beach on Tulabi Lake used as a boat launch, then turn right to take the unmarked lakeside trail. If the campground is closed, you'll have to walk in from the gate (about 15 minutes), but this also offers more privacy and thus is well worth the effort. Northern Hawk Owls can sometimes be seen along this gravel road.

For the unmarked 1.5 km (0.9 mi.; one-way) trail near the Flanders Lake cottages, take Flanders Lake Rd., just past the road that goes up to Tulabi campground, turning south/right off Bird Lake Rd. About 250 m/yds past the turnoff to the Flanders Lake Block 1 cottages, but on the opposite side of the road (on the left), is a small trail running into the woods. The offshoots are all worth exploring and fairly short, but to get to the main trail to the Black Spruce swamp described in the text above, avoid the right-hand trail that runs parallel to Flanders Lake Rd. (20 m/yds from the trailhead) and instead go straight for about 650 m/yds before turning left.

26

OSTENFELD

OSTENFELD IS A small agricultural community 43 km (27 mi.) east of Winnipeg. Settled by Danish immigrants around 1925, the landscape is a mosaic of small farms and northern aspen parkland complemented by a rich abundance of marshland and other wetland types. This provides for a diversity of bird species that prefer deciduous-dominated treed habitats, patchy habitats, and wetlands. It's a good example of the flat but rich-soiled habitat remaining after Lake Agassiz, the enormous glacial lake left following the retreat of glaciers at the end of the last ice age, drained away about 8,000 years ago. Ostenfeld is close to the transition zone from parkland to boreal forest. While most of the birding opportunities described here are in Ostenfeld, to extend your birding day you can also add a 50 km

A female Golden-winged Warbler perches in her preferred deciduous habitat.
RYAN MCDONALD

drive east to Elma. This drive crosses a range of habitats, from wetlands and agricultural fields to Jack Pine– and Red Pine–dominated forest, and thus is known locally for providing opportunities to see a diversity of bird species. Ostenfeld offers a very special but easily overlooked birding opportunity: Golden-winged Warblers, which are found in just a couple of populations in Canada. Sadly, this exquisitely pretty warbler is declining at an alarming rate. One reason for this is their fairly specific preference for early-successional deciduous forest, particularly within a broader forest matrix. The natural mosaic of grassland and deciduous forest historically typical of northern aspen parkland was strongly dependent on disturbance from wildfires. Without fires, forest patches in the region quickly age past the successional stage preferred by Golden-winged Warblers and are rarely replaced with more recently disturbed habitats. Consequently, a variety of species that inhabit early successional habitats, such as Chestnut-sided Warbler, Prairie Warbler, Eastern Whip-poor-will, and Golden-winged Warbler, are in decline.

Golden-winged Warblers also face a more unusual threat: hybridization with the Blue-winged Warbler, a closely related species. Prior to European colonization, these two species were mostly geographically isolated from each other, but habitat fragmentation through forest clearing created new opportunities for Blue-winged Warblers to move into Golden-winged Warbler habitat, and the two species began to interbreed more regularly where their populations overlapped. For some reason as yet unknown to scientists, Blue-winged Warbler genes quickly swamp those of the

is where Brewster's Warblers have made their homes in the past, becoming neighbours to the Yellow Warblers, Black-and-white Warblers, Black-billed Cuckoos, Baltimore Orioles, and Rose-breasted Grosbeaks that also occur here. Interestingly, this is also a site where Yellow-throated Vireos have been known to occur.

The drive from Ostenfeld or Winnipeg to Elma along Old Hwy. 15 offers good winter birding opportunities as a result of the mix of wetlands, deciduous and Black Spruce/Tamarack forests, and agricultural fields intersected by the road, and the feeders at private homes within Elma itself. Spruce Grouse and Northern Hawk Owls can be found within or adjacent to the coniferous and mixed forests along the drive. Black-backed and American Three-toed Woodpeckers occur primarily in the coniferous forests. This route is also a good place to spot Snowy Owls, Great Horned Owls, and Snow Buntings. Other species that occur in the winter near the highway or at feeders in Elma include Common and a few Hoary Redpolls, Evening and Pine Grosbeaks, Boreal Chickadees, and Purple Finches.

GETTING THERE

To get to the Ostenfeld Golden-winged Warbler forest patch, take Hwy. 15 from Winnipeg (also signposted as Dugald Rd. and Route 115 within city limits) east through Dugald and Anola to PR 302 south (take the gravel road on the right-hand/south side of the highway, not the paved road on the left, which is also called PR 302). Turn right (south) toward Ostenfeld and travel 11 km (7 mi.) along PR 302, until the road ends at a T. PR 302 continues east (to your left), while

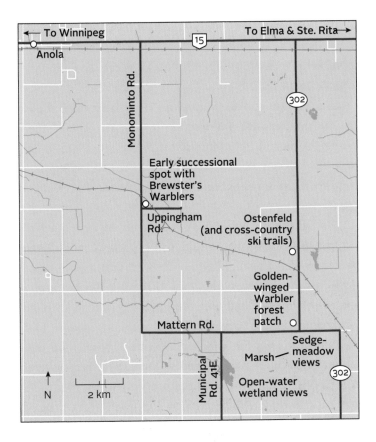

Mattern Rd. is west (to your right). The forest patch is on the northwest corner of this intersection.

A large marsh is located immediately south of PR 302/ Mattern Rd. but can't be seen from this intersection. For a view of the grass- and sedge-dominated section, turn east/ left on PR 302 from the junction with Mattern Rd., for about 50 m/yds; the wetland is on your right (south side of the road). For open-water species, turn west on Mattern Rd.

from the junction with PR 302, and travel 3.2 km (2 mi.) to Municipal Rd. 41 East (sign says MUN 41 E). Turn left and travel on 41 E about 500 m/yds, to a large open pond on the left side of the road.

To access the Ostenfeld rail line, drive west from the PR 302 and Mattern Rd. intersection for 6.4 km (4 mi.), then turn right (north) onto Monominto Rd. and drive for 5 km, past Uppingham Rd. to the rail line. Brewster's Warblers have been known to occur east of Monominto and north of Uppingham.

Most of the Ostenfeld area is privately owned, but birders can use cross-country ski trails upon a municipally owned gravel esker if, like me, they feel that a day of birding just isn't complete without a nature walk. Trails are very wet at the lower elevations, but gradually ascend through aspen-dominated to bur oak forest, providing diverse birding opportunities. The trails are abundant, broad, and well maintained but unmarked, and walkers must keep careful note of their route to ensure they can eventually find their way back to their vehicle. The trail location is not marked from the road, either. The easiest way to find these trails is to go to the rail line that crosses PR 302 along the north side of the Ostenfeld Church property, and continue 1 km (0.6 mi.) north of this rail line on PR 302 to an open, mowed field on your left (west side of the road) with a small spot where you can park. Walk along the north side of the open field to its northwest corner, then head south for about 10 m/yds along the west side of the field, until you're immediately west of where you parked. The trail entrance into the forest can be seen here. (Note: Wood Ticks and mosquitoes are often very abundant; dress appropriately.)

To get to Elma, take Hwy. 15 east from Winnipeg (or from Ostenfeld, go north on PR 302 to Hwy. 15, and then turn east). For best birding opportunities, turn south onto Old 15 (13 km/8 mi. east of Ste. Rita, and 8.2 km east of the sign for Agassiz Provincial Forest); after about 0.5 km, follow the road as it turns east to stay on Old 15. Stop at the willow-dominated wetlands, grassland patch, and Black Spruce/Tamarack forests to seek out habitat-specialist species. Elma is 90 km east of Winnipeg, but add an extra 20 minutes' driving time if following Old 15.

Unlike in most bird species, phalarope eggs are incubated by the male parent (here, a Wilson's Phalarope), and thus the male is the duller-coloured sex, to avoid attracting predators while on the nest. ILYA POVALYAEV

27

OAK HAMMOCK MARSH

OAK HAMMOCK MARSH is one of the best-known birding destinations in southern Manitoba, and its reputation for diverse birding opportunities and high-quality facilities is well deserved. It's widely appreciated for its inviting native-grass green-roofed nature centre and dozens of square kilometres of restored wetland, although its high-quality remnants of tall-grass prairie receive much less attention. While it protects an impressive 3,600 ha (8,900 acres) of wetlands and uplands, this represents only a fraction of the 47,000 ha (116,000 acre) St. Andrews bog that occurred here historically. Originally drained for agricultural purposes, wetland restorations have been ongoing since 1972. Because the hydrology of the landscape has been so dramatically altered over the last century, the marsh depends on active management via the intensively engineered dike system. Adjacent uplands complement the wetlands, and as a result this diverse landscape attracts a tremendous abundance and diversity of birds.

BIRDING GUIDE

Wetlands are legitimately the focus of the Oak Hammock Marsh Wildlife Management Area. Nonetheless, the initial few metres of uplands before entering the trails offer an abundance of birding opportunities. Purple Martin houses are occupied by a healthy population of the species, and the skies are full of other aerial insectivores such as Tree, Barn, and Bank Swallows. Killdeer often nest in the gravel south of the parking lot, providing an up-close birding opportunity that will be exciting to kids and adults alike, and uplifting to even the most experienced birder who's seen it all before. Shrubs and emergent vegetation surrounding the beautifully designed boardwalk and gravel trail system are teeming with Swamp Sparrows and Marsh Wrens. This is a great location to see Yellow-headed Blackbirds, which occur here toward the edge of their range and thus are much less abundant than in the other Prairie provinces. Shorebirds and waterfowl are too numerous to list, but include significant populations of favourites such as Black-bellied Plovers, Short-billed Dowitchers, Wilson's Phalaropes, Ruddy Ducks, and Northern Pintails. Great and Cattle Egrets also occur occasionally. The nature centre itself has an impressive observation deck overlooking the marsh, offering a particularly interesting perspective in the pre-dusk period when vast mixed-species flocks settle in the wetlands to roost.

Don't overlook the uplands that intersperse the wetland trail network. A gazebo houses a large colony of Barn Swallows. While sheltering there for a picnic is not recommended (due to risk of droppings), the experience in June of being surrounded by swallows flitting in and out to forage and feed their young is not to be missed. The wet meadows surrounding the wetlands are regularly used by Sedge Wrens, Nelson's Sparrows, and LeConte's Sparrows, though these are more likely to be heard than seen.

The tall-grass prairie west of the nature centre is often ignored, but is well worth a visit. At over 350 ha (860 acres), it's one of the largest and best-quality remaining representations of this critically endangered ecosystem in this region. In May and June it's heavily used by grassland birds. Savannah Sparrows, LeConte's Sparrows, and Western Meadowlarks are abundant, while Sharp-tailed Grouse and Sedge Wrens may also be detected. Bobolinks occur here regularly, but in lower densities than in some other locations within the province; indeed, they may be more abundant in the adjacent hayfields. Birds become harder to locate by mid-July, when breeding activity slows, a typical issue with birding in prairies anywhere. However, the flowers are so abundant and diverse in the summer that it still provides a pleasant stroll and you may flush up some fledglings while walking. Yellow Rails may be heard at night from the wetlands on the north side of the Brennan prairie, a much wetter property just northwest of this tall-grass prairie.

Oak Hammock Marsh occasionally offers a public bird-banding program that provides a unique opportunity to see a variety of different species in the hand—a completely different experience from field birding. Banding at Oak

Hammock Marsh focuses on passerines and allies; common species captured include Tree and Barn Swallows, Yellow-rumped (Myrtle's) Warblers, Common Yellowthroats, Swamp Sparrows, and many migrants passing through in the spring and fall. Call 204-467-3300 or check the website for banding dates (oakhammockmarsh.ca).

Oak Hammock Marsh is located within a key migration flyway, and is one of the best locations in the province for watching all types of avian migrants in the spring and fall. Migrant shorebirds are abundant and diverse. Many raptors and passerines also migrate through, including Palm Warblers, American Redstarts, American Tree Sparrows, Fox Sparrows, Harris's Sparrows, and White-crowned Sparrows. There are vast numbers of ducks and geese here during the spring and fall migration periods. In the winter it's a great place to see Snowy Owls, Lapland Longspurs, and Snow Buntings, while the visitor centre provides much-appreciated respite from the cold.

GETTING THERE

There are a couple of possible routes from Winnipeg. Both take about 30 minutes. You can take Route 90 (Century St.) north until it turns into Hwy. 7. Drive for 26 km (16 mi.) on Hwy. 7, then turn east onto Hwy. 67 for 8 km, and then north onto PR 220 for 4 km. Alternatively, take Hwy. 8 north for 19 km, and then turn west onto Hwy. 67 and go west for 6 km, before turning north on PR 220. The Marsh is well signed starting from the northbound highways. PR 220 ends at the nature centre, which you can't miss.

For the best of the two tall-grass prairie remnants at Oak Hammock, instead of turning right into the nature centre

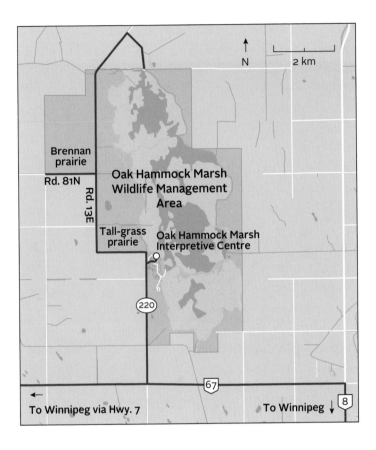

parking lot, drive past it. Soon, this gravel road makes a
sharp left turn. Follow this road west for about a kilometre—you're now driving along the south side of the tall-grass
prairie. The road ends at a T. Turn right. You'll see a tiny
parking lot for the tall-grass prairie on your right at an interpretive sign. To access the wetter Brennan prairie, continue
north from this parking lot for about 2.5 km (1.6 mi.), and
turn left onto Rd. 81 N. The Brennan prairie is the section on
your right and is signposted.

Usually most easily seen perched atop fence posts, Upland Sandpipers produce a call that sounds like a wolf whistle. BARBARA BLEHO

28

MANITOBA TALL GRASS PRAIRIE PRESERVE

THE MANITOBA TALL Grass Prairie Preserve (MTGP) protects over 2,000 ha (5,000 acres) of tall-grass prairie, Bur Oak–poplar savanna, wetlands, and small patches of poplar-dominated forest. Well over 99% of Manitoba's tall-grass prairies have been sacrificed to our agricultural goals since European colonization of the region. The largest clusters of native tall-grass prairies remaining in the province occur in the MTGP and its surrounding regions. These prairies owe their survival not only to their rocky soils, which made cultivation difficult, but also to the management strategy of prescribed burning brought by Ukrainian and other European farmers who settled this part of the province, which has proven critical for the conservation of this disturbance-loving ecosystem. The MTGP is managed by a consortium of governmental and non-governmental agencies working together to conserve this endangered ecosystem. Prescribed burns remain an important active management strategy.

The MTGP is home to numerous endangered and threatened species. The Western Prairie Fringed Orchid (easy to spot along the Agassiz Trail) and Small White Lady's-slipper, for example, both occur in the preserve. Poweshiek Skipperling and Dakota Skipper butterflies, both of which have suffered alarming declines over recent decades, occur here. Sadly, the Poweshiek Skipperling, found nowhere else in Canada, is facing imminent threat of extinction. Several bird species at risk are regularly found in the MTGP during breeding season, including Yellow Rail, Short-eared Owl, Eastern Whip-poor-will, Red-headed Woodpecker, and during migration, Canada Warbler and Olive-sided Flycatcher.

Many other bird species can also be found here, of course. Manitoba is currently experiencing a climatically wet cycle, and gradual recent changes in the bird community have reflected this naturally occurring environmental change. Species that prefer wet meadows and shrubs, such as LeConte's Sparrows, Clay-colored Sparrows, Wilson's Snipes, Yellow Rails, and Common Yellowthroats, have become more numerous here over the last decade, while grassland specialists such as Bobolinks and Savannah Sparrows have declined in abundance. Nonetheless, the preserve remains a mosaic of grasslands, forests, and shallow wetlands, providing numerous opportunities for observing a diversity of bird species. Specific locations that are suitable for different species will vary according to moisture levels.

BIRDING GUIDE

The preserve consists of a patchwork of properties loosely clustered into the North Block and the South Block (to the north and south of PR 201 respectively). The public can access most sections on foot from the adjacent roadways. And three interpretive trails, Agassiz and Prairie Orchid (North Block) and Prairie Shore (South Block), offer good access to tall-grass prairie, sedge meadow, and aspen parkland habitats. The Weston Family Tall Grass Prairie Interpretive Centre is located in roughly the centre of the preserve, adjacent to the Prairie Orchid Trail, and provides information on tall-grass prairie conservation and natural history.

While grasslands, shrubs, forests, and wetlands can be found throughout the preserve, in general, the most northern sections are relatively wet, although little standing water is easily seen from roads or trails. Here, there is abundant moist habitat for wetland-loving species such as Marbled Godwit, Yellow Rail, Virginia Rail, Sora, American Bittern, and Nelson's Sparrow, and wet-meadow species including Sedge Wren and LeConte's Sparrow. Eastern Whip-poor-wills also occur here. The larger patches of tall-grass prairie in both blocks provide habitat for a range of grassland species, including Upland Sandpiper, Savannah Sparrow, Bobolink, Western Meadowlark, Sharp-tailed Grouse, and Vesper Sparrow, and their relatively moist current condition means that wet-meadow and wetland species are also found here regularly, including Sedge Wren and Wilson's Snipe. The most southern portions of the preserve tend to be shrubby, thus providing good habitat for Common Yellow-throats, American Goldfinches, and Lark Sparrows, as well as grassland and forest species. Northern Rough-winged

Swallows can be seen near the bridge over the Roseau River on Purple Bank Rd., near the intersection with PR 209. Deciduous forest patches throughout the preserve provide habitat for a wide variety of species that are particularly amenable to field birding, including Eastern Towhee, Rose-breasted Grosbeak, Indigo Bunting, American Redstart, and a few Golden-winged Warblers. Northern Harriers and Sandhill Cranes are also abundant in the region.

The preserve is an important site both for breeding birds and for migrants passing through in the spring and fall. Almost all the species mentioned above regularly breed in the preserve. Species commonly found during migration include many warblers, such as Tennessee, Palm, Blackpoll, Wilson's, and Orange-crowned; sparrows such as Fox, American Tree, and Lincoln's; Lapland Longspurs; and water birds such as Red-necked and Eared Grebes, Wilson's Phalaropes, and Semipalmated and Least Sandpipers, among many others. Other occasional visitors have included Great Egrets, Red-bellied Woodpeckers, Field Sparrows, and Orchard Orioles.

GETTING THERE

The MTGP is approximately 100 km (62 mi.) south of Winnipeg, just east of Hwy. 59. From Winnipeg, the Weston Family Tall Grass Prairie Interpretive Centre and its adjacent Prairie Orchid Trail can be accessed by turning east/left from Hwy. 59 onto PR 201; pass through Stuartburn, and then turn north onto PR 32 E and follow the signs. The interpretive centre is primarily open in the summer and early fall; days and times vary. For up-to-date information, call the centre at 204-425-8118.

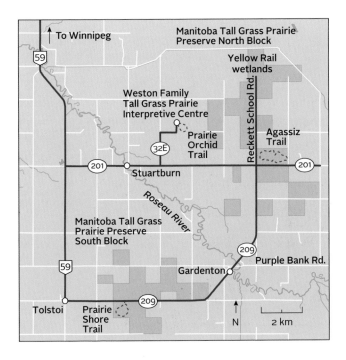

To reach the Prairie Shore Trail, continue south along Hwy. 59 for 6.7 km (4.1 mi.) past the turnoff to PR 201, until you get to the community of Tolstoi. Turn east/left onto PR 209 in Tolstoi. The Prairie Shore Trail is on the south side of the road, 3 km east of Tolstoi.

To reach the northern blocks where Yellow Rails can be found, take the PR 201 turnoff east from Hwy. 59. Turn north onto PR 209 (known locally as Reckett School Rd.). Travel north for about 4 km (2.5 mi.), until the road jogs left. The Yellow Rail wetlands are to the north of this corner (but note that conditions on this road can be poor).

Active management and conservation efforts have helped to recover Peregrine Falcon populations across Canada. ILYA POVALYAEV

29

WINNIPEG

IN OUR DESIRE to interact with nature and its inhabitants, we often overlook wildlife that we see every day. This makes it easy to forget about the birds that live among us in our urban centres. Manitoba's cities and towns typically have abundant green spaces and urban forests that provide habitat for a multitude of species. Winnipeg, for example, has many diverse birding opportunities, as its forest, garden, and riparian habitats provide a unique island of resources embedded within its surrounding oceans of agriculture. Thus, this city has become both a critical stopover point for migrating birds and a magnet for species both typical and atypical of the prairies. Species in cities benefit from protection from some predators, additional food sources, and the "heat-island" effect, as cities tend to be several degrees warmer than rural habitats. This may explain the occurrence of several surprising accidental species found in Winnipeg in the last few years, including a pair of Mississippi Kites that nested in the River Heights neighbourhood of Winnipeg in 2014. Winnipeggers can easily access many different habitat types across the city, and thus can find diverse birding opportunities right on our doorsteps.

BIRDING GUIDE

Each region of the city has its own bird community, which changes with the seasons. Peregrine Falcons, here from late March or April through August, love the "artificial cliffs" created by skyscrapers—a pair usually nesting on or near the Radisson Hotel is filmed annually and can be viewed live by streaming the "Falcon Cam." Once listed as Endangered, Peregrine Falcon populations have increased steadily across Canada in recent decades and are now considered federally as Special Concern. Another interesting urban species at risk is the Chimney Swift, which is abundant across the older parts of the city. Chimney Swifts are easiest to spot when entering their nesting or roosting chimneys around sunset during migration and the breeding season. One consistently inhabited chimney is that of Assiniboine School in St. James.

The Red, Assiniboine, and Seine Rivers provide extensive ribbons of green riparian habitat across the city, and many wonderful parks are associated with these areas. Among these is King's Park, toward the southern end of the city. Hooded Mergansers and Mallards frequent its ponds. Along the forested riverside trails, here and across the city, Wood Ducks nest and form small, colourful flocks. Common species breeding in or near the park include Downy and Hairy Woodpeckers, American Robins, White-breasted Nuthatches, House Finches, Song Sparrows, American Goldfinches, and Barn, Cliff, and Bank Swallows. Eastern Screech-Owls have a strong affinity for riparian areas of moderately high human density within Winnipeg. One hypothesis to explain this pattern is that these smaller owls find a safe refuge in parks near humans because larger owls avoid humans.

There are also several smaller parks scattered across Winnipeg that protect important remnants of the tall-grass prairie ecosystem that historically reached from here to Oklahoma. One of these easily overlooked little urban parks is the George Olive Nature Park, at just 6.5 ha (16 acres). The park includes a tiny restored tall-grass prairie and a 3 ha (7 acre) wetland that has remarkable species diversity despite its diminutive size. American Coots, Ruddy Ducks, Yellow-headed and Red-winged Blackbirds, Western King-birds, Warbling Vireos, American Goldfinches, Barn Swallows, and Killdeer all use this tiny patch of natural habitat; even Pied-billed Grebes have been known to breed here. Another relatively hidden tall-grass prairie remnant is protected by the New Tall Grass Prairie Preserve (for-merly Rotary Prairie Nature Park). Surrounded by industrial development, it isn't much to look at from the road, but it protects a nice patch of tall-grass prairie and is home to LeConte's Sparrows, Red-winged Blackbirds, Savannah Sparrows, Western Meadowlarks, Clay-colored Sparrows, Killdeer, American Goldfinches, and others. Better known is the larger Living Prairie Museum and Park. In addition to its great interpretive centre, this park protects 12 ha (30 acres) of remnant tall-grass prairie. Despite being surrounded by residences and a school, the prairie is managed using an impressive rotational prescribed burning program and thus its quality is remarkable, despite its relative isolation from other prairies. Clay-colored Sparrows, Savannah Sparrows, Western Meadowlarks, Barn Swallows, and occasionally LeConte's Sparrows are found in the prairie, while the adjacent forest is inhabited by Long-eared Owls and other species.

Assiniboine Park is Winnipeg's best-known green space, and it's widely used for diverse recreational purposes throughout the year. Less heavily used by humans is the adjacent Bur Oak– and poplar-dominated Assiniboine Forest. Together, the park and forest protect over 700 ha (1700 acres) in the centre of the city. In the park, birding opportunities are best within the Assiniboine Park Zoo, the Leo Mol Sculpture Garden, and the English Garden, where Ruby-throated Hummingbirds are often seen. Numerous species are seen regularly in the park, including Wood Ducks, Great Blue Herons, and Hooded Mergansers in the ponds; Pileated Woodpeckers and Warbling and Blue-headed Vireos in the treed patches; and Cooper's and Sharp-shinned Hawks, Merlins, and owls, including Long-eared, Great Horned, Eastern Screech-Owls, and Northern Hawk Owls. During migration, Palm, Wilson's, and Orange-crowned Warblers, Lincoln's and Lark Sparrows, Pied-billed Grebes, Northern Shrikes, and many other species occur throughout the park and forest. Great Crested Flycatchers (near the English Garden), Indigo Buntings, and Rose-breasted Grosbeaks may breed here or move through during migration. Assiniboine

Forest provides a wide range of trails. Choose a loop that swings by the marsh, which has a helpful viewing mound on its west side. Birding in Assiniboine Forest is best during migration, when numerous passerines and water birds move through. Species that breed in Assiniboine Forest include Least Flycatchers, Eastern Phoebes, Yellow-bellied Sapsuckers, and American Redstarts; Nashville, Black-and-white, Magnolia, and Yellow Warblers; Red-winged Blackbirds; and Northern Saw-whet Owls. Short-eared Owls, Wilson's Snipes, and American Woodcocks sometimes occur in open grassy patches within the forest matrix.

Residential areas, too, can offer wonderful birding opportunities. Older neighbourhoods tend to have a greater diversity of vegetation types and heights; thus, bird diversity tends to increase as neighbourhoods age. During the breeding season, Merlins are abundant throughout the city. Clay-colored Sparrows and Savannah Sparrows can be found in shrubby or grassy roadsides and abandoned lots, and Chipping and Song Sparrows, and Purple and House Finches, can be found in the elms and boulevard trees. Pine Siskins occur in small groups of coniferous trees. While many neighbourhoods have a diversity of birds, communities near the rivers, such as West Broadway, tend to be particularly diverse. Indigo Buntings, Red-breasted and White-breasted Nuthatches, and Pileated Woodpeckers all breed in the West Broadway area. It's also heavily used by migrants in the spring and fall. These often include massive flocks of Hermit Thrushes, and other regular migrants include Scarlet Tanagers; Blackburnian, Magnolia, Tennessee, Nashville, Yellow, Black-and-white, Black-throated Green, and Orange-crowned Warblers;

Ruby-crowned and Golden-crowned Kinglets; and American Redstarts, Harris's Sparrows, and Rose-breasted Grosbeaks, among many others.

GETTING THERE

The Radisson Hotel is at 288 Portage Ave., at the corner of Portage Ave. and Smith St. Assiniboine School is on Winston Rd., just south of Portage Ave., about 5 km (3 mi.) west of the Radisson Hotel.

King's Park is off Kings Dr. From Pembina Hwy., take Dalhousie Dr. east to Silverstone Ave. Turn left/east onto Silverstone, then right onto Kings Dr.

To get to George Olive Nature Park, take Dugald Rd. east from central Winnipeg, toward Transcona. Turn left/north onto Ravenhurst St., which turns into McMeans Ave. East. George Olive Nature Park is on the northeast side of this road. The New Tall Grass Prairie Preserve is 7 km (4.3 mi.) from George Olive, on the north side of Regent Ave. West in the 1200 block, just west of Bienvenue St.

To get to the Living Prairie Museum, from Portage Ave. take Sturgeon Rd. north, then take the third street on the right onto Ness Ave. The Living Prairie Museum is one block east of Sturgeon Rd., on the north side of Ness Ave.

Assiniboine Park is on the north side of Roblin Blvd., while Assiniboine Forest is immediately south of the park on the south side of Roblin Blvd., both west of the intersection with Shaftesbury Blvd. There are useful maps of the park available at assiniboinepark.ca, or follow signs to the English and Sculpture Gardens once in the park.

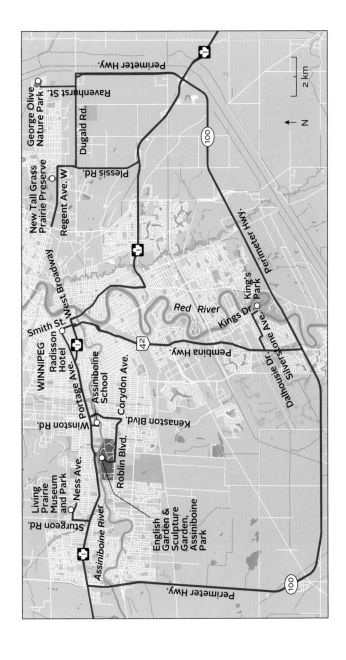

A Greater Yellowlegs plunges into an icy lake. ILYA POVALYAEV

—30—
BEAUDRY PROVINCIAL PARK AND FORTWHYTE ALIVE

BEAUDRY PROVINCIAL PARK and FortWhyte Alive, both just west of Winnipeg, each protect a mix of grasslands, forest, and aquatic habitats, many of which reflect the successes of decades-old habitat restoration activities. While either makes a nice visit on its own, for a full day of birding in the spring try an early start in Beaudry Provincial Park for the prairie dawn chorus, followed by looping southeast to FortWhyte for a picnic or lunch in the café, and then a search for water and forest birds around the extensive managed lake system.

Beaudry Provincial Park protects 950 ha (2,350 acres) of forest, river, and prairie habitats. It is best known for its cross-country ski trails and is much less well used in the spring, summer, and fall, possibly due to sometimes spectacular abundances of mosquitoes and ticks. Its best characteristic is the 120 ha (300 acre) restored tall-grass prairie located at its heart. Formerly cultivated lands here were seeded with tall-grass prairie seeds starting in 1987, and the prairie is often mowed and occasionally burned to maintain its quality. Trails wind through the grassland and riparian forest, providing diverse birding opportunities.

Habitat restoration and reclamation activities began at former clay and gravel pits at Fort Whyte in the 1950s, and the site facility, now named FortWhyte Alive, has been actively managed for wildlife conservation ever since. It's a great example of the tremendous successes that intensive restoration actions can achieve once enough time has passed to allow the goals of conservation visionaries to be realized. The grassland components are mostly exotic plants or are of fairly low plant diversity, and so their bird communities typically aren't quite as diverse as in native prairies at other sites, but during migration check for Sandhill Cranes and Broad-winged and Rough-legged Hawks. The southern portion of FortWhyte, starting at the Alloway Reception Centre, has a great trail system winding throughout its patchwork of forests, wetlands, and lakes, and thus birding here is a lot of fun.

BIRDING GUIDE

Beaudry's best feature during the breeding season is its often abundant Bobolink population. While a few other sites in Manitoba are also home to Bobolinks, most of them provide views only from roadsides or are colonized in some years but not others. At Beaudry, birders can easily access the centre of the large prairie, and in late May and June can get relatively close to a number of singing and displaying Bobolinks. Prairie birds are particularly sensitive to time, and are much more active first thing in the morning, quieting down around 9:00 or 10:00 a.m. So, start morning hikes on the trail that winds through the prairie, gradually make your way to the forested Elm Trail or Wild Grape Trail, and head back to the parking lot from there. In the prairies you can also find Sharp-tailed Grouse; American Goldfinches; Clay-colored, Vesper, Savannah, and LeConte's Sparrows; and Killdeer, Eastern Kingbirds, and Western Meadowlarks. Brewer's Blackbirds sometimes flock here. Yellow Warblers, American Redstarts, Least Flycatchers, Red-eyed Vireos, White-throated Sparrows, Ovenbirds, Rose-breasted Grosbeaks, Black-and-white and Tennessee Warblers, Great Crested Flycatchers, and owls, including Northern Hawk Owls, breed in the surrounding forests. This is also a great park to look for migrants in the spring and fall.

All the trail options at FortWhyte Alive are well maintained and offer abundant birding opportunities. You may choose to start birding on the south deck of the Alloway Reception Centre. Use this vantage point to scan Lake Devonian for waterfowl. In the spring and summer, Hooded Mergansers, Wood Ducks, Pied-billed Grebes, and American White Pelicans are likely, while Great Egrets and Black-crowned Night-Herons occur more rarely. Greater White-fronted and Snow Geese occur here occasionally during migration, while Tundra Swans, Gadwalls, American Wigeons, Northern Pintails, and both Lesser and Greater

Scaups are regular migrants. After this, pass through the interpretive centre building, making a quick stop at the Prairie Partners exhibit to check out some live Burrowing Owls, housed here in collaboration with the Manitoba Burrowing Owl Recovery Program and Assiniboine Park Zoo.

South of the interpretive centre, take the Waterfowl Garden Trail for a mix of deciduous forest and small wetlands. While Soras are heard at many wetlands across Manitoba, FortWhyte's trail system passes by these wetlands closely enough that it's a good spot to try to see them as well. American Coots are also likely here, while Virginia Rails occur occasionally. American Bitterns typically pass through during migration. The deciduous forest supports a wide range of different species during the breeding season, such as Hermit and Swainson's Thrushes, Gray Catbirds, Yellow Warblers, Baltimore Orioles, Least Flycatchers, and a variety of woodpeckers. Many less-common species may also be found here during the breeding season, including Yellow-bellied and Great Crested Flycatchers (more likely closer to water bodies), Eastern Wood-Pewee, Orchard Orioles, Yellow-throated and Philadelphia Vireos, Black-billed Cuckoos, Scarlet Tanagers, Eastern Screech-Owls, and Great Horned Owls. Follow the signs along the forest trail to the bird feeders for some up-close sightings of forest songbirds and woodpeckers. The forests at FortWhyte Alive are full of exciting and surprising discoveries during migration periods, and residents are fairly abundant in the winter.

Alternatively, follow the signs for the Wetland Boardwalk Trail and the Lakeside Trail around Muir Lake. In addition to the lake-dwelling species mentioned above, during the migration periods look for Common and Red-breasted

Mergansers, Ruddy Ducks, Red-necked and Western Grebes, Black Terns, and Greater and Lesser Yellowlegs. Belted Kingfishers, Common Yellowthroats, Spotted Sandpipers, and Marsh and Sedge Wrens; Tree, Bank, Barn, and Cliff Swallows; and Double-crested Cormorants, Eastern Phoebes, and Eastern Kingbirds are all likely at or near the lakes during the breeding season.

GETTING THERE

Beaudry Provincial Park is about 10 km (6 mi.) from the edge of Winnipeg. Take Roblin Blvd. West, which changes to PR 241 at the perimeter of the city, right to the park. The Wild Grape Trail leaves straight from the parking lot. For the prairie trails, backtrack slightly along the road that goes to the parking lot, heading south; the prairie will be on your right (west). Wander along the prairie trails roughly north; at the north end of the prairie, you can hook up with the Elm Trail, and then turn right to head back to the parking lot while birding through the forest habitat. (Note: Mosquitoes can be extremely dense in the forests here in the spring and summer.)

To get to FortWhyte Alive from Beaudry Provincial Park, head back east toward Winnipeg along PR 241. Then turn south on the Perimeter Hwy. for 10 km (6.2 mi.), then northeast/left onto PR 155 for 7 km (this road will turn into McGillivray Blvd). Following the signs to FortWhyte Alive, turn north/left from PR 155 onto McCreary Rd. and proceed 1 km, until you see the entrance sign to FortWhyte Alive on your right. If you're coming from central Winnipeg, head southwest on McGillivray Blvd. Do not take the group entrance road access at 2505 McGillivray, but continue

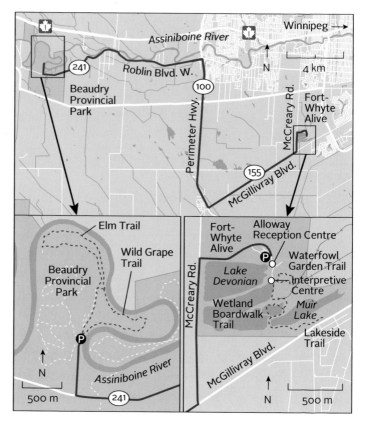

driving and turn right onto McCreary Rd. and follow the directions as above.

Admission prices to FortWhyte Alive range up to $8 per person if you drive there, but admission is free if you arrive on foot or by bike; for more information, check their website at fortwhyte.org. After passing through the Reception Centre (where you can pick up a map), Lake Devonian will be on your right and the interpretive centre is straight ahead. From there, follow the trail signs to your preferred trail.

—31—

RIDING MOUNTAIN
NATIONAL PARK

RIDING MOUNTAIN NATIONAL Park is an almost 300,000 ha (740,000 acre) island of natural habitat surrounded by an ocean of agriculture. Along its eastern border rises the Pembina Escarpment (often known as the Manitoba Escarpment), which was protected from glacial erosion by the layer of shale that contributes to the mountain's elevation. The centre of the park is conifer-dominated mixed-wood boreal, transitioning to deciduous forest to its east and eventually to a mosaic of forest and grasslands to the west. This park provides outstanding birding opportunities throughout the year.

Riding Mountain is heavily used by tourists from June through September, with fewer visitors in May and October.

The park facilities are closed November through April, although many trails can still be accessed; this results in some inconvenience but also a marvellous sense of privacy. The park provides some of the best winter birding in southern Manitoba, with abundant White-winged Crossbills, Ruffed and (fewer) Spruce Grouse, Great Gray Owls, and American Three-toed, Black-backed, and other woodpeckers.

BIRDING GUIDE

Numerous trails (off Hwy. 10 and Hwy. 19, both within the park) provide access to conifer-dominated boreal forest, and all are worth visiting. The Boreal Trail is a pretty and easy (but not wheelchair accessible, despite its label on some park maps) gravel and boardwalk trail winding across a creek and through edges of forest along this wetland. It's good for many species, including Boreal Chickadees, Lincoln's Sparrows, and Cape May Warblers. The Brûlé Trail passes through stands of a range of successional stages, including very small patches of dry meadow, a rare habitat type that is at risk across the boreal forest due to fire suppression. The dry meadows on this trail are home to the rare Macoun's Arctic butterfly, a tiny, biennial butterfly that emerges briefly in odd years and depends on meadows surrounded by Jack Pine for its reproductive activities. The Whirlpool Lake parking lot area provides access to numerous habitat types and thus is also an excellent focal point for birding. The parking lot area itself is conifer dominated and promising

◀ The Canada Warbler is one of our country's Species At Risk. ILYA POVALYAEV

for Boreal Chickadees and Brown Creepers, among others. The first 400 m/yds or so of the Cowan Lake Trail, which starts here, are deciduous-dominated and provide habitat for many early successional species, including Black-and-white Warblers and Nashville Warblers. Over the next 600 m/yds, this trail transitions to conifer dominated, and 1 km (0.6 mi.) from the trailhead the habitat becomes primarily coniferous and is a great spot to look for American Three-toed and Black-backed Woodpeckers. If you're here in the evening in the early spring, stop in open, grassy areas along Hwy. 19 to check for American Woodcocks.

The east side of the park is home to what is probably the most genetically pure population of Golden-winged Warblers in the world. This species has been declining rapidly throughout its range, in part because of interbreeding with Blue-winged Warblers (for more information on this species see Ostenfeld, pages 175–76). To see Golden-winged Warblers and numerous other deciduous-forest species, including American Redstarts, Nashville Warblers, and more rarely Red-headed Woodpeckers, Indigo Buntings, Scarlet Tanagers, and Eastern Towhees, try the Bur Oak– and poplar-dominated Oak Ridge Trail. Both the road and the trail provide good birding opportunities.

Birding during spring and fall migration is excellent throughout the park, but particularly along the forested berm between South and Clear Lakes. Ideally, arrive early in the morning to take advantage of both morning bird activity and the relative lack of human visitors along this busy trail, and park at the tiny parking lot for the South Lake Trail. Walk 1.6 km (1 mi.) north along a gently winding mixed-wood trail to the Clear Lake South Shore Trail, and turn left along the trail. You'll almost immediately arrive at a narrow berm of land that provides views of wetlands to the south, open water to the north, and forest along the berm for several kilometres. All these habitats provide outstanding opportunities to see a wide variety of migrants. Scan the shoreline for shorebirds such as Spotted Sandpipers, and the open water for flocks of ducks such as Ring-necked Duck, Mallard, and rarely, American Black Duck and White-winged Scoter; geese such as Snow and Greater White-fronted; and Tundra Swans. During migration, flocks often consist of mixed species, so look at all individuals to make sure you don't miss something exciting. Look south/left to South Lake for Sora, Blue-winged Teal, Green-winged Teal, and Ruddy Duck, although during migration these waterfowl may also be found on the bigger water bodies. Forest and shrubs along the berm are magnets for migrating passerines of all kinds, including many warblers that primarily breed elsewhere (e.g., Blackpoll, Palm, and Wilson's), and many sparrows. Water birds will start passing through in the spring as soon as the ice is out (April or May), and can be found again from late summer until ice-up (late November), while passerines pass through in waves of different species, peaking in May and September. As a result, it's worth visiting this spot several times per season. On the walk back to your vehicle, you'll have more time to enjoy the lovely 1 km boardwalk on the Ominnik Marsh Trail. Keep an eye out for Marsh Wrens, Common Yellowthroats, and Soras.

If you want more privacy than found around Clear Lake, Proven Lake, just south of the national park, has recently been named an Important Bird Area. It's a large (2,000 ha/ 5,000 acres) marsh surrounded by mixed poplar–Black Spruce forest, and some agricultural activity. The trail passes along a dike, which provides excellent viewing opportunities of both open water and a managed waterfowl pond. The lake is an important staging area during migration and is well known for colonies of nesting Black-crowned Night-Herons, Eared Grebes, and Franklin's Gulls. Many other species also breed here, including Great Blue Herons, American Bitterns, Black and Forster's Terns, Hooded Mergansers, Ruddy Ducks, and Marsh and Sedge Wrens.

GETTING THERE

To get to the main south park entrance from Winnipeg, take Hwy. 1 west for 86 km (53 mi.) from the Winnipeg Perimeter Hwy. (Hwy. 100). After Portage la Prairie, turn north onto Hwy. 16 for 116 km, then north onto Hwy. 10 in Minnedosa, and stay on Hwy. 10 for 50 km. The birding opportunities in and around the potholes and lakes along this stretch can be great if you take a somewhat longer drive along one of the smaller provincial roads that run more or less parallel to Hwy. 10.

Numerous pleasant trails start directly at Hwy. 10 within the national park. The Boreal Trail is 27.5 km (17 mi.) north of the Hwy. 19 turnoff. For the Brûlé Trail and Whirlpool Lake parking lot, go north on Hwy. 10 from the south entrance of the park, and east/right on Hwy. 19 (a gravel road). The turnoff to the Brûlé Trail is about 2 km east of Hwy. 10 along Hwy. 19, while the turnoff to the Whirlpool Lake is about 10 km east of the junction with Hwy. 10; the Whirlpool Lake Rd. itself is about 3 km long.

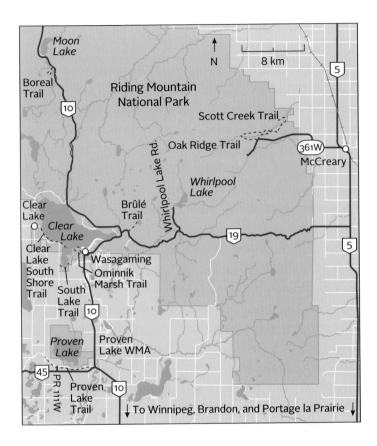

For the Oak Ridge Trail, drive east on Hwy. 19 for 20 km (12.4 mi.) from the turnoff to Whirlpool Lake, at which point you'll exit the park. Then continue another 5 km east to Hwy. 5. Turn left/north onto Hwy. 5 and drive for 10 km, then turn west on PR 361 W. This road turns north and then west. After 6.7 km it re-enters Riding Mountain National Park. The Oak Ridge trailhead is 4.5 km west from the park boundary. After 600 m/yds, the trail itself branches right, along the Scott Creek Trail, and left, toward the Oak Ridge

Trail loop. Scott Creek Trail typically has higher abundances of Golden-winged Warblers.

Signage to the South Lake Trail, Clear Lake South Shore Trail, and Ominnik Marsh Trail can be confusing. Travel north on Hwy. 10 from the south entrance into the park. About 500 m/yds from the south entrance, turn west/left at the sign for Clear Lake and Wasagaming. Take the first left, Mooswa Dr., and then continue past the intersection with Wasagaming Rd. Mooswa Dr. turns into Boat Cove Rd. at this point. Down the hill and on your left you will see a small parking lot with a tiny sign pointing to Ominnik Marsh Trail. Park here. Walk from here, following the sign to Ominnik Marsh Trail, along the road, about 50 m/yds. On your left you'll see a large interpretive sign about Ominnik Marsh, and a tiny sign for South Lake Trail. Walk up the South Lake Trail for 1.6 km (1 mi.). South Lake Trail ends at a T with Clear Lake South Shore Trail (also called Lakeshore Trail, South Shore Clear Lake Trail, and Clear Lake Trail). Turn left at this T; you'll almost immediately reach the berm between Clear Lake and South Lake, and can now bird at your leisure. In theory you can walk for 25 km around the perimeter of Clear Lake (not all of it is maintained); most birders will stick to the first several kilometres along the south shore. On the way back you can check out Ominnik Marsh Trail; to get there, return to South Lake Trail and head south on foot. About 1 km from the junction with Clear Lake South Shore Trail, take the right-hand trail from which you can see the viewing platform and boardwalk. From here you can do the Ominnik Marsh Trail backwards, returning to the South Lake Trail after about 1 km along the boardwalk. Turn right (south) to return to your car.

To get to Proven Lake, start at the south entrance of the national park, and travel south along Hwy. 10, out of the park. Drive 14.5 km (9 mi.) to Hwy. 45 and turn right (west), then immediately turn right again at the first gravel road to your right, along PR 111 W. Drive 5.2 km along this gravel road to the trailhead, at which there is a large sign for Proven Lake.

Bald Eagles in the shallows. ILYA POVALYAEV

32

OAK LAKE AND PLUM LAKES

THE OAK AND Plum Lakes Important Bird Area in south-west Manitoba is a mosaic of shallow, cattail-fringed marshes that provide breeding habitat for many species and critical staging habitat for migrating waterfowl. Native and planted trees and grazed pastures and haylands in the surrounding uplands provide additional complementary habitat, resulting in an abundance of birding opportunities in this area. Perhaps the best part is the dike running southwest from Oak Lake Beach, between Oak Lake on the northwest side and Plum Marsh on the southeast side, which provides excellent viewing opportunities of shrubs, haylands, open water, and cattail marshes. You can drive on the dike, but be sure not to block the roadway at either end when you park. As with most open-water birding, a spotting scope is desirable, though not essential.

Colonies of Franklin's Gulls, Eared Grebes, Black-crowned Night-Herons, and American White Pelicans occur here during breeding season. Other breeding water birds include Gadwall, American Wigeon, Blue- and Green-winged Teal, Ruddy and Ring-necked Ducks, Sora, and Virginia Rail. Wilson's Snipes winnow along the wetland fringes. Both Eastern and Mountain Bluebird occur in the adjacent uplands, along with Black-and-white Warbler, Brewer's Blackbird, and Eastern Wood-Pewee. Bobolinks often occur in nearby haylands, while Grasshopper Sparrows, LeConte's Sparrows, Vesper Sparrows, Upland Sandpipers, Sprague's Pipits, and Sharp-tailed Grouse occur in nearby grasslands. A colony of Purple Martins lives near the eastern shore. Deciduous-treed sand dunes in the surrounding region provide good habitat for Eastern Towhee, Warbling Vireo, and Least Flycatchers.

The site also provides excellent viewing opportunities during migration, including good abundances of Greater White-fronted Geese, Snow Geese, Tundra Swans, and Bald and Golden Eagles. A wide variety of waterfowl also migrate through here, including Long-tailed Ducks and White-winged Scoter. Sandhill Cranes occur in surrounding agricultural fields in large numbers, where Rough-legged Hawks will also pass through or overwinter.

BIRDING GUIDE

During the peak songbird breeding season, from late May through early July, take advantage of an early morning visit by starting along the woodlands in Oak Lake Provincial Park, a tiny park within the Oak Lake region. Birds sing most actively between about a half hour before dawn and 9:00 or 10:00 a.m., and their vocalizations can be used to locate and identify individuals, particularly after leaf-out in the spring. This provincial park includes a small and heavily disturbed forest, which nonetheless provides habitat for breeding Great Crested Flycatchers, Eastern Wood-Pewee, Rose-breasted Grosbeaks, and Orchard and Baltimore Orioles. Many additional species can also be found here during migration.

After this, turn south along Lakeshore Dr. and travel along the top of the dike for the best opportunity to spot water birds. Gray Catbirds and Yellow Warblers occur in the trees and shrubs on either side of the trail. Ducks, geese, and swans are typically more abundant in the open water of Oak Lake, to your right, but also occur in the wetlands on the southeast side of the dike, on your left, along with American Coot. Listen for LeConte's Sparrows and Sedge Wrens in the wet meadow adjacent to the dike, and Nelson's Sparrows and Marsh Wrens among the cattails themselves. American Bittern, Black-crowned Night-Heron, Sora, and Wilson's Snipe also occur within the marshes along the dike.

After an enjoyable few hours birding in the provincial park and along the dike, you'll probably be ready for a picnic lunch. While numerous pleasant spots are available, I particularly like the south-facing bench adjacent to the Cherry Point Educational Nature Trail, just down the little hill from the parking lot, on the northeast side of the lake. Abundant shrubs and trees provide habitat around this little nature trail, and Savannah Sparrows are likely in the meadow. Other grassland species may be found in pastures on the north side of Cherry Point Rd. and east of PR 254.

While driving to this site, watch for Sharp-tailed Grouse along the roadsides. Loggerhead Shrikes are possible close to Hwy. 83. Raptors such as Swainson's Hawks, Red-tailed Hawks, Ferruginous Hawks, and Northern Harriers may be seen during this drive in the spring and early summer, while Rough-legged Hawks will migrate through and may over-winter here.

GETTING THERE

From Winnipeg (279 km/173 mi.) or Brandon (69 km), travel west along Hwy. 1 and then turn south onto PR 254 for 10 km; the alternative route along Hwy. 2 is 5 km longer for Winnipeg, 17 km longer for Brandon, but offers better birding opportunities.

Start at Oak Lake Beach for forest birding if you arrive early in the morning. To reach the dike from here, turn left/south on Lakeshore Dr. The dike begins about 800 m/yds from here. You can drive or walk the additional 5 km (3.1 mi.) to the dam that interrupts the dike.

To get to the Cherry Point Educational Nature Trail, head back up Lakeshore Dr. to the provincial park. Continue straight ahead (north), passing the provincial park on your right. After about 3 km (1.9 mi.), turn left onto Cherry Point Rd. This road turns into Oak Ave. 800 m/yds from the junction with PR 254. The nature trail and its parking lot are located on your left off of Oak Ave., after you pass the small Cherry Point subdivision, about 1.5 km west of PR 254.

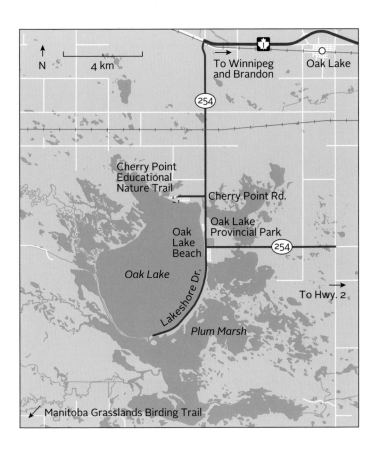

33

WHITEWATER LAKE

WHITEWATER LAKE IS a rare endorheic lake (without a natural outlet) that's only up to about 3 m (10 ft.) deep and thus provides a unique habitat for a wide variety of water birds. It's an Important Bird Area and well known locally as a major hot spot for a variety of species, some found in few or no other locations in the province. It's also highly controversial. As it lacks an outlet, it ranges from entirely dry to flooding thousands of hectares of surrounding farmland. A proposal to build two outlets to stabilize water levels and reduce overland flooding has pitted landowners against conservation organizations. The dispute was ongoing at the time of writing.

◀ American Avocets can be identified by their gorgeous plumage and upturned bill. ILYA POVALYAEV

The lake and its surroundings have changed tremendously in recent years. Flooding has badly degraded dikes built by Ducks Unlimited Canada, and the marsh trails and boardwalk associated with the Whitewater Lake Wildlife Management Area (WMA) are now impassable, perhaps irretrievably. The viewing mound may now be impossible to reach. Nonetheless, the lake still provides exceptional birding opportunities. It's a critical staging area for migratory birds, and also provides a home for many breeding species. The grasslands, trees, and wetlands around the fringe of the lake also provide abundant habitat for species such as Marbled Godwit, Willet, and shorebirds that require short vegetation; Eastern and Western Kingbirds, Eastern Bluebirds, and Orchard and Baltimore Orioles; and Horned Larks in the short grasses and Bobolinks in the tall grasses. Therefore, much attention should be paid on the drive and walk in toward the lakeside.

While the variety of species found at Whitewater Lake is far too long to list in full here, some highlights include breeding colonies of White-faced Ibis; Eared, Western (and Clark's, rarely), and Pied-billed Grebes; Great, Snowy, and Cattle Egrets; and Black-crowned Night-Herons. Glossy Ibis are rare but becoming more regular. Least Bitterns have occurred here, as do accidentals such as Yellow-crowned Night-Herons, Little Blue Herons, and Tricolored Herons. During migration, Osprey and Golden Eagles also pass through. The lake is known for huge flocks of American Avocets during migration, as well as Stilt Sandpipers, Short-billed and Long-billed Dowitchers, Dunlins, Ruddy Turnstones, and sometimes Whimbrels and Red Knots, among many others.

BIRDING GUIDE

Whitewater Lake wma is a good starting point, despite recent degradation by flooding. On the drive toward the wma, watch for birds in the surrounding grasslands and agricultural fields. Shallowly flooded fields and pastures can be particularly good in late July and August for Arctic-breeding shallow-water species. The parking lot can no longer be reached by vehicle (ironic, I know), so park in front of the barrier. The wetlands adjacent to the trail here are good for Marsh and Sedge Wrens, Soras, White-faced and possibly Glossy Ibis, and various grebes, possibly including Clark's. This spot offers good views of both the marshes and open water, and may lead to views of Black and Forster's Terns, more grebes, and numerous duck species, egrets, and sandpipers. During migration, this site is a good spot to observe flocks of Tundra Swans, Snow and Greater White-fronted Geese, and Snow Buntings in late fall in the former parking lot.

It's also worth seeking out several other viewpoints along the lake. After driving away from the wma, take your first right (15 N), drive west 1 km (0.6 mi.) until the road turns south again (becoming 124 w), and stop. This corner, formerly far from the water's edge, now provides good views of open water, cattail fringe, and some open muddy edges, and thus a chance to see a few more species. Here and elsewhere, please stay on the road rights-of-way as surrounding properties are privately owned. After, drive to the west side of the lake. In the fall and winter, there may be Snowy Owls along this drive. The roads to the west of the open water are surrounded by cattail-fringed wetlands including large open ponds, providing additional excellent viewing opportunities. At the municipal road 15 N, you can park and then walk in toward the lake about 1.5 km; alternatively, for less walking, you can continue to drive north on 132 w for 1.6 km, then go east on 16 N for 1.6 km, and then south about 1 km to end up close to this point, but with a slightly different viewpoint. Golden and Bald Eagles may be seen in this area during migration. You may also want to pop over to the north side of the lake for more views of flocks that may use open water, and the now distant, inaccessible Sextons Island.

GETTING THERE

Pay attention to your own position relative to the cardinal directions here, as many signs in this area have been knocked sideways or turned 90°, or are otherwise misleading.

From Winnipeg, travel to Boissevain west along Hwy. 2 (219 km/136 mi.) and then south on Hwy. 10 (44 km). From Boissevain to the Whitewater Lake viewing platform, take PR 15 N, which lies immediately to the south of town (the sign may be sideways and it may look, incorrectly, as if you will be travelling along Old #3 or 115 w). Turn west/right onto PR 15 N. After 1.6 km, turn south/left onto 116 w, and follow the road when it turns west onto 14 N. Drive about 11 km, then turn right on 123 w, following the signs to the Whitewater Lake WMA. The stretch from Boissevain to the WMA is good for Loggerhead Shrikes, Brown Thrashers, and raptors including Ferruginous Hawks.

After checking out the sights at the WMA and in the surrounding agricultural lands, head back south on 123 w, but take the first right (west) onto 15 N (sign may be sideways and instead say 123 w). Drive 1.6 km (1 mi.), until the road turns south/left; this corner is your second stopping point. From

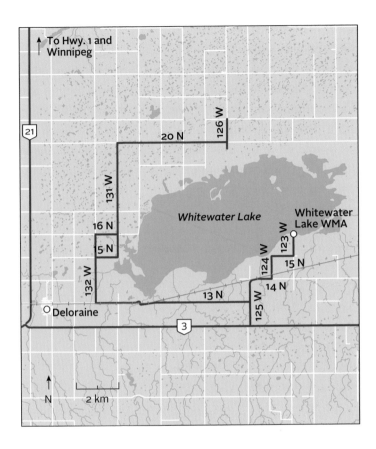

here, follow the road to head south on 124 w for 1.6 km, turning right (west) immediately after crossing the railway tracks, onto 14 N (sign may be turned). Continue west on 14 N for 1.6 km and then follow the road as it turns south/left onto 125 w. Go south 1.6 km then turn right onto 13 N, and travel along this road for 11 km, to skirt the southern edge of the lake.

To take a look at the western shore, turn north/right from 13 N onto 132 w. Travel for 3.2 km (2 mi.) through the cattail marshes and open water, stopping to bird at the larger ponds of open water. You can then park along 132 w to walk east/right along 15 N, or go another 1.6 km north, then drive east on 16 N for 1.6 km, then south on 131 w as long as the road conditions are good. To head up to the northern shore and a view of Sextons Island, turn 180° to face north on 131 w, and drive 4.8 km and turn right onto 20 N. Drive 6.4 km east, then turn south onto 126 w and drive 1.6 km up to the bend in the road.

34

MANITOBA GRASSLANDS BIRDING TRAIL: NORTHERN ROUTE

THE SOUTHWEST CORNER of Manitoba used to be home to massive plains of mixed-grass prairies, but only tiny remnants remain. Over the last century, most of these grasslands have been converted to cropland, but others have been lost because of the extirpation of vast herds of Plains Bison and Pronghorn, and control of wildfire, which historically kept much of the habitat at a grass-and-forb-dominated early successional stage. In the absence of abundant native grazers and fire, most of the habitat in this moist and productive region quickly succeeds to forest, and thus many properties protected from further development also quickly lose value to the threatened and endangered

Male Chestnut-collared Longspur returns to his nest to feed his nestlings.
JENNIFER HORVAT

grassland-specialist species found in this area. Cattle grazing is now necessary for the conservation of many species here.

The importance of this region to grassland birds has been recognized through the development of the Manitoba Grasslands Birding Trail, which brings the observer to up to 13 viewing points along a 183 km (114 mi.) driving route. The four locations described here provide opportunities to observe many of Manitoba's mixed-grass prairie birds, both at the stopping points and along the driving route. For a longer visit to the area, the whole Birding Trail is recommended, or visitors can stop at Oak and Plum Lakes or Whitewater Lake if heading back east toward Winnipeg.

BIRDING GUIDE

Grassland songbirds are easiest to find during the breeding season, from late May through June, when singing and aerial displays aid in locating them. Days with little wind and no precipitation are best. There's also more bird activity once ambient temperatures reach at least 5°C (41°F), but things quiet down once hot temperatures are reached, by 9:00 or 10:00 a.m. Start as early as possible in the morning at the Broomhill Wildlife Management Area (WMA) for a glorious spring morning walk through this grassy prairie. Start in the quarter-section on the west side of the road, which has fewer shrubs than the east side and thus is best for the pickiest of our grassland species; however, the whole WMA is well worth a longer walk. Threatened Sprague's Pipits and provincially endangered Baird's Sparrows, as well as Vesper Sparrows, Western Meadowlarks, Bobolinks, and Upland Sandpipers may be found in the grasslands here. Although endangered Burrowing Owls have been spotted here in the past, the grass is now taller, denser, and generally less suitable for this species. Species that use the shrubs here include the provincially endangered Loggerhead Shrike, a carnivorous passerine that impales its prey on thorns or barbed-wire fences to facilitate handling and to cache for later use. Willow Flycatcher and Say's Phoebe may also occur here, while Swainson's Hawks and the provincially endangered Ferruginous Hawk may include the WMA in their large home-ranges. Sharp-tailed Grouse occur here regularly, and a lek, where numerous males gather to display and attract mates, has also been located here. For a chance to see the Sharp-tailed Grouse display lek, get here as early as possible in the morning in late April or early May, and listen for coos and cackles to identify the lek location. Stay well back to avoid disturbing the birds.

The next spot to visit is the Mixed-grass Prairie Preserve (MGPP), about 17 km (10.5 mi.) from the Broomhill WMA. This patch of prairie is thought to have never been cultivated, an unusual occurrence in Manitoba. It's actively managed with grazing cattle, which are crucial for maintaining its early successional grassland conditions. The preserve itself is therefore fenced off and cannot be entered, but an unused grassy road allowance along its south border provides a good opportunity for a walk to find more grassland birds. Sprague's Pipits are likely, Baird's and Grasshopper Sparrows possible, and because this site is grazed, it's also promising for Chestnut-collared Longspurs, a provincially endangered species.

Next, drive south through an area known locally as the Poverty Plains, named for the economic devastation of the dust-bowl years. Many farms were initially cultivated and then abandoned during the drought of the mid- to late 1930s, leaving the landscape to slowly recover to its original mixed-grass prairie habitat. While it will take hundreds of years for these properties, known locally as "go-back prairies," to recover to pre-cultivation conditions, they now provide critical habitat for many grassland species. Here and throughout the driving route, Northern Harriers, Ferruginous Hawks, Loggerhead Shrikes, and Upland Sandpipers are all possible. Short-eared Owls, provincially threatened, are rare but seen occasionally. The gravel road south of the MGPP is worth frequent stops to seek out grassland birds. Look for the largest grassland patches with the fewest shrubs and trees for sensitive grassland species at risk, such as Chestnut-collared Longspurs and Sprague's Pipits. Grasshopper Sparrows have an unusual habitat preference for tall grasses but abundant bare ground; as a result, they may be present where exotic perennial grasses such as Crested Wheatgrass has been planted in rangelands. Chestnut-collared Longspurs prefer heavily grazed vegetation, while Sprague's Pipits and Baird's Sparrows prefer taller grasses, so stop alongside both types of grasslands.

Finally, a stop at the Gerald W. Malaher WMA provides an opportunity for a very different stroll along its well-maintained, extensively interpreted trails. A small wetland has been dammed, and numerous exotic and native trees and shrubs planted, providing locally unusual habitats that attract a range of species such as Pied-billed Grebes, Hooded Mergansers, Gray Catbirds, Cedar Waxwings, and Great Horned and Long-eared Owls. Many species use the WMA during migration. It's also a particularly good spot in this prairie region for winter birding, providing habitat (in some years) for Common and Hoary Redpolls, White-winged Crossbills, and Pine Grosbeaks—and look for Snowy Owls during the drive there.

GETTING THERE

To start at the Broomhill WMA, head north on Hwy. 83 from Melita; then turn left onto PR 345. Alternatively, from Winnipeg, take Hwy. 2 to Hwy. 83; turn left (south) onto Hwy. 83 and drive about 18 km (11 mi.) to PR 345, then turn right. Broomhill WMA is about 320 km from Winnipeg. From Brandon, you can get to this intersection by travelling south on Hwy. 10 for 25 km; then turn west onto Hwy. 2 for 76 km, and then south on Hwy. 83 to PR 345, where you will turn west.

From the Hwy. 83/PR 345 intersection, head west on PR 345 for 4.9 km (3 mi.). You'll see signs for the Broomhill WMA on your right; turn right at this gravel road and drive north for 0.8 km, to the small parking area (note the Manitoba Grasslands Birding Trail sign on your left). This is the northwest quarter-section at which to start your walk.

To get to the Mixed-grass Prairie Preserve, head back to PR 345, turn west/right, and drive for 11.7 km (7.3 mi.); then turn south/left onto PR 165 W. Drive 4.9 km along this road until you see the MGPP sign on your left. Park along the road, and walk up the unused road allowance that runs along the south side of the MGPP (24 N). After visiting the Mixed-grass Prairie Preserve, drive south along 165 W through the Poverty Plains.

To get to the Gerald W. Malaher WMA, drive 10 km (6.2 mi.) south of the MGPP and turn east onto PR 445. Drive

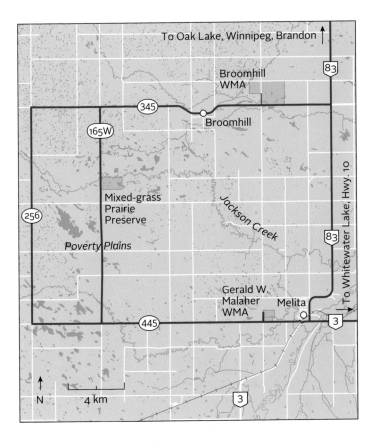

11.5 km east, where you'll see a sign for the WMA. Turn north/left up the gravel road that runs along the west side of the WMA, and start your hike from the parking lot on your right.

35

HECLA/GRINDSTONE PROVINCIAL PARK

ECLA/GRINDSTONE PROVINCIAL PARK protects over 100,000 ha (247,000 acres) of boreal habitat on peninsulas and islands that emerge into Lake Winnipeg, including extensive forests, wetlands, and lakeshore, providing outstanding and varied birding opportunities. As is typical of large points of lands surrounded by massive water bodies, it can be a magnet during migration for all types of birds. Lake Winnipeg is one of the last water bodies in the area to ice up near shore in the late fall, and thus can offer the best birding in the region at this time, attracting abundant fish-eating water birds such as Red-breasted and Hooded

◀ Three-toed and many other species of woodpecker thrive in Hecla/Grindstone Provincial Park. ILYA POVALYAEV

239

Mergansers, Osprey, many grebes, and Bald and occasionally Golden Eagles. Indeed, Hecla Island is well known for attracting vast numbers of Bald Eagles during fall migration, resulting in a quite spectacular sight of massive flocks of the raptor.

Hecla has more tourism facilities, such as trails, than Grindstone, and thus is the focus of this description. For a longer trip or just a different scene, birding near the cottage community in Grindstone can also be rewarding.

BIRDING GUIDE

Grassy Narrows Marsh is a massive (1,000 ha/2,470 acres) wetland running along the southwest corner of Hecla Island. Despite intensive hydrological management, the cattails have really taken hold of these wetlands. However, some substantial open ponds remain. Views of the open water, to seek out all sorts of ducks including Northern Pintail, Gadwall, Green-winged Teal, Redhead, Ring-necked Duck, and White-winged and occasionally Black Scoters during migration, are quite good from Hwy. 8 and from the road leading to the Grassy Narrows trails. There are a variety of trails to choose from, some of which involve a fair bit of walking adjacent to relatively unproductive cattail. Among the moderately long trails, Bittern Trail, at 6.5 km (4 mi.) round-trip, passes by relatively high proportions of open ponds. Chorus Frog, at just 0.6 km one-way, provides a pleasant, diverse walk, passing through alder and poplar thickets (check for Alder Flycatchers, Eastern Kingbirds, and Yellow Warblers) to a covered, floating platform offering excellent views of a large pond.

A different view of the marsh can be obtained from the wildlife viewing platform, which is a 500 m/yd walk off Hwy. 8, several miles northwest of the rest of the Grassy Narrows trails. Unfortunately there's little standing water visible from the platform, so you'll need to listen for American Bittern, Sora, and Alder and Yellow-bellied Flycatchers, and watch for raptors such as Northern Harriers and possibly Broad-winged Hawks hunting above the wetlands.

The other trails are at some distance from Grassy Narrows, toward the north end of Hecla Island. They are all more or less interconnected and have a range of access points. West Quarry Trail consists of a 3.5 km (2.2 mi.) loop plus an approximately 4 km one-way trail connecting with a campground. The loop passes through mixed-wood Balsam, spruce, ash, and poplar forest and alongside a wetland. A rundown but functional gazebo provides great views of the wetland and the treed, rocky berm between the wetland and Lake Winnipeg proper. It's also well worth walking the pretty 1.2 km trail to the end of the wetland; from here, you can look for birds in the wetland, along the berm, and on the open water. Canvasbacks, Blue- and Green-winged Teal, Ring-necked Duck, and Ruddy Duck may be present in the wetland. Trees along the berm should be checked for migrant passerines in the spring. The forested portions of the trail provide habitat for Ruffed and Spruce (more commonly encountered in the winter) Grouse, Boreal Chickadees, Golden- and Ruby-crowned Kinglets, and Pileated and other woodpeckers. More deciduous patches within the forest may contain American Redstarts and Nashville and Orange-crowned Warblers. Many passerines will be found here during spring and fall migration. The trail may be accessed both from a parking lot adjacent to the loop portion, and from the opposite end at the campground, where Boreal Chickadees are particularly abundant.

The Sunset Beach Trail offers a range of different possibilities, depending on how much time you have. It's only 250 m/yds from the parking lot through a winding, forested path to the rocky but beautiful beach. As the name suggests, the sunsets viewed from here are stunning. Walk the 750 m/yd loop through the mixed-wood forest, or connect from Sunset Beach Trail to North Point Trail (also called Hamars Lake Trail), which offers up to 12.5 km (7.8 mi.) of further trail options (and also a loop of about half that distance). The Hamars Lake Trail can also easily be accessed from the parking lot at the end of Hwy. 8, from the Gull Harbour Marina, and from Lakeview Hecla Resort. The conifer-dominated forest near Sunset Beach provides habitat for American Three-toed and Black-backed Woodpeckers, Veery, Swainson's and Hermit Thrushes, and Blackburnian and occasionally Bay-breasted Warblers. Black-throated Green and, rarely, Black-throated Blue Warblers have also been recorded on Hecla Island. During migration, Blackpoll and Palm Warblers; Lincoln's, American Tree, Harris's, and Fox Sparrows; and Red Crossbills pass through. Hamars Lake Trail opens up to the North Point picnic site with its widely spaced birches; occasionally, Baltimore Orioles may be seen here. Hamars Lake Trail continues east and south from the picnic site, along the east side of North Point.

Several spots around Gull Harbour offer good opportunities for seeing open-water species. Off the coast of Hecla Island are numerous colonies of water birds, including Double-crested Cormorants, American White Pelican, Herring

Gulls, and Caspian Terns. Bonaparte's and Franklin's Gulls and Forster's Terns are seen here often. Flocks of Tundra Swans, and Snow and Greater White-fronted Geese pass through during migration, particularly in the fall, as do mixed flocks of ducks—check for American Black Ducks, Greater Scaups, Red-breasted Mergansers, and Barrow's Goldeneyes, all of which occasionally or rarely pass through and may be mistaken for more common species (Mallards, Lesser Scaups, Common Mergansers, and Common Goldeneyes, respectively). The best location for viewing open-water birds varies with wind, season, and where fish are schooling, but several spots are often rewarding. Among these are the Gull Harbour Marina, east portion of Hamars Lake Trail, and North Point picnic site. The latter has a very high viewing platform, where a spotting scope would be useful. Perhaps the best option, though, is the 2.5 km (1.6 mi.) round-trip Lighthouse Point Trail, starting either at the Gull Harbour Beach or the Lakeview Hecla Resort, which provides excellent opportunities for viewing water birds, as well as Pileated and other woodpeckers throughout the year, and Bald Eagles during the fall migration.

GETTING THERE

Hecla Island is easy to get to from Winnipeg; simply drive north on Hwy. 8 for 170 km (106 mi.) from the junction with Winnipeg's Perimeter Hwy. Hwy. 8 ends in Gull Harbour, at the north point of the island. Most of the trails described here start in this area, except for the Grassy Narrows Marsh trails, which are about 30 km southwest of here (closer to Winnipeg) along Hwy. 8.

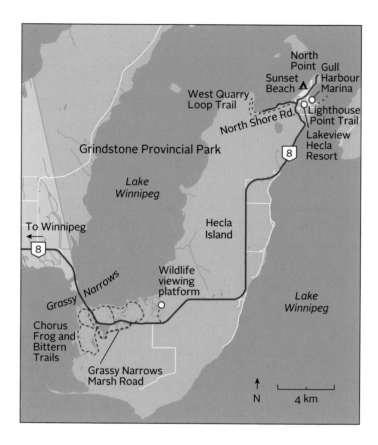

To get to Grassy Narrows Marsh starting at the south end of the island (i.e., the point on the island that is closest to Winnipeg), look for the sign for Grassy Narrows Marsh on the right-hand (south) side of the road, right after the causeway entering the park but well before the park-pass hut. The gravel road to the parking lot is about 2 km (1.2 mi.) long. For the Chorus Frog Trail, turn right over the red bridge at the end of the parking lot. Bittern Trail can be accessed from

Chorus Frog; follow the coloured signs along the trail. The Wildlife Viewing Platform Trail is accessed from a different parking lot, located 5.5 km farther along Hwy. 8 after the turnoff for the Grassy Narrows Marsh trails.

To get to the West Quarry Trail loop, drive about 24 km (15 mi.) past the causeway entering the park. Turn left on North Shore Rd., which ends at the parking lot for the trail loop. To start at the opposite end of the West Quarry Trail, pass the turnoff for North Shore Rd. and instead turn left into the campground. You'll see the sign to West Quarry Trail on your left, 150 m/yds from the campground gate.

Hamars Lake Trail can be accessed from several points. A good option is to park at the marina to first scan the open water, then turn north (left, if you're facing the water), past the Lighthouse Inn and a couple of cottages, and onto the trail. Alternatively, drive along Hwy. 8 past the marina and park in the parking lot for Sunset Beach, which is on the left-hand side of the road. To go to Sunset Beach or along the Sunset Beach loop, turn right at the trail's T-junction 70 m/yds from the trailhead, then left at the next trail junction. To access the Hamars Lake Trail, turn right instead of left at the second junction, following the symbol for the picnic area. A final option is to simply drive to and park at North Point, which is at the end of Hwy. 8, 400 m/yds beyond the turnoff for Sunset Beach.

The Lighthouse Point Trail starts near the northeast corner of Lakeview Hecla Resort, or at the southeast corner of the Gull Harbour Beach, which is a short walk (across Hwy. 8) from the campground.

Willow Ptarmigan, shown here, and Rock Ptarmigan can both be found around Churchill. ILYA POVALYAEV

36

CHURCHILL

BY RUDOLF KOES

RRIVING IN CHURCHILL for the first time, by plane or
by train, is an eye-opener for prairie birders. The rugged landscape, with its rocky headlands, tundra, and
stunted trees, is dramatically different from any other
site in this book, and thus provides access to a unique avian
community. The completion of a railway line to Churchill
in 1929 opened up this area to ornithologists, who discovered, among many other species, the first nests of Harris's
Sparrow. In the 1960s, amateur birders started to visit. The
discovery of a Ross's Gull in 1978, and the subsequent nesting of this species from 1980 on, brought scores of birding
tour groups and individuals to the area, which led to more
discoveries. In recent decades, rarities such as Common

Crane, Ruff, Black-headed Gull, and White-winged Tern have added to Churchill's allure. Accidentals from the south or west, such as Little Blue Heron, Band-tailed Pigeon, Rufous Hummingbird, Violet-green Swallow, and Rock Wren have also been found here.

But Churchill is especially inviting as a place to get close to shorebirds in glorious breeding plumage and to view a variety of sea ducks, jaegers, and gulls. One little-known fact about it is that it's tied with the Niagara River for having hosted the largest number of gull species (20) in a single location anywhere in the world. It's certain to create lifetime memories for birders lucky enough to make the long trip from Winnipeg.

BIRDING GUIDE

To do this area justice, allow at least four days, preferably between early June and mid-July. Later in the season the variety of bird species lessens and biting insects become an increasingly significant nuisance, although those interested in seeing Beluga Whales or wildflowers may prefer July or August. Polar Bears are big business in town, with the season running from October to November (when Gyrfalcon, Snowy Owl, Rock Ptarmigan, and some ducks and gulls may also be seen), but sightings are possible in summer.

There are many locations worth visiting, but for me, some stand out from the rest. The mouth of the Churchill River at Cape Merry is typically the number one spot. Not only is the scenery spectacular, with Prince of Wales Fort looming on the far bank, but the birding here is at once exciting and relaxing. Few things in life are more pleasurable than spending a few hours sitting in the sun and out of the wind on the rocks near the tip of Cape Merry, while enjoying the flocks of Common Eiders, scoters, and Long-tailed Ducks, or watching a Parasitic Jaeger in action as it harasses Arctic Terns carrying small fish to their nearby nests. The first Beluga Whales of the season usually start arriving in early June, and later in the season Harlequin Ducks and Black Guillemots may be present. Be sure to check the Granary Ponds next to the grain elevator on your way to or from Cape Merry. This site offers good opportunities for close viewing of ducks and shorebirds, especially if you remain in your vehicle.

Next on the recommended itinerary is Goose Creek/ Hydro Rd. Ponds along the road attract ducks and shorebirds, the latter sometimes in the thousands during migration. Here you'll get a chance to hone your identification skills, as numerous species often mingle close by, especially south of the Goose Creek crossing. The marshy area immediately north of the bridge is home to American Bittern, Gray-cheeked Thrush, and Nelson's Sparrow, plus a host of other species. Be sure to also visit the weir to the west of this area, or the pumphouse at the end of the road, where views of the river may turn up something of interest. With luck you'll spot a Sabine's Gull or Long-tailed Jaeger flying by, and Little Gulls are likely in the area. Finally, a few feeders in the Goose Creek cottage subdivision usually attract Harris's Sparrow, redpolls, and Pine Grosbeak.

The Churchill Northern Studies Centre (CNSC), a state-of-the-art research and educational facility, provides further excellent birding opportunities. It's well worth a visit, and if your timing is right, you can enjoy a delicious meal and mingle with researchers, students, and birders. Patches of tundra along the road to the centre are likely to produce American Golden-Plover and Whimbrel. Past the centre, the road turns south and takes you past the remnants of the former Churchill Rocket Range. Keep your eyes open for Willow Ptarmigan. After several kilometres along this bumpy track you'll reach a large, open, wet tundra area, the Big Fen. Make frequent stops, as this is a great area to scan for shorebirds. To the south, mature coniferous forest starts and trails lead to both East and West Twin Lakes. These forests provide your best chances of seeing Spruce Grouse, American Three-toed and Black-backed Woodpeckers, Gray Jay, Boreal Chickadee, Bohemian Waxwing, several species of warbler, and White-winged Crossbill. Although the likelihood of meeting a Polar Bear is slim during the birding season, always be alert and aware of your surroundings.

GETTING THERE

Various birding tour operators conduct tours of Churchill, and the Churchill Northern Studies Centre offers a birding course (learning vacation) in early June. You can also arrange a visit on your own. However you choose to do it, it's vital to follow Polar Bear safety protocols when there's even the smallest risk of Polar Bears being present.

There are no roads into Churchill. Visitors must either fly from Winnipeg or take the train (which takes 36 hours). Alternatively, you can drive to Thompson (about 760 km/470 mi.) and take the overnight train from there (about 16 hours).

You need a vehicle in Churchill, as distances are too great to cover on foot. There are no car-rental agencies in town,

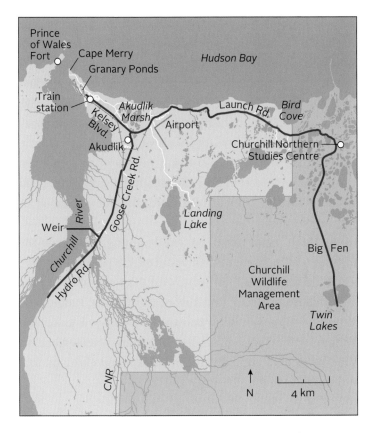

but many locals and some hotels rent out trucks. Participants in organized tours and those taking the birding course at CNSC will be driven around.

From the airport, Kelsey Blvd. (locally known as "The Highway") leads to town. To reach the Granary Ponds, continue through town until you see the elevators on your left. The ponds are opposite the elevators and on your right, next to the road. Continue to a curve, where the road climbs a steep hill, go right around an old bunkhouse, and follow the signs to Cape Merry.

Goose Creek Rd., and its extension Hydro Rd., can be reached by returning toward the airport, but turning right (south) at Akudlik Marsh. The Goose Creek cottage subdivision is several kilometres down this road and is well marked. Just past here, the road dips down toward a productive marsh area. A dike to the right leads to the weir. Continuing on, you'll cross the two channels of Goose Creek. Immediately past the second crossing is access to a marina; washrooms are located here. Beyond the crossings the road becomes known as Hydro Rd., with the pumphouse at its terminus.

To reach CNSC, return to The Highway, drive past the airport, and continue east for about 20 km (12.4 mi.), where The Highway turns into Launch Rd. It's impossible to miss the modern building and the nearby rocket range. The extension of Launch Rd. is known locally as Twin Lakes Rd., although it's not signed as such. There are several tracks in the Twin Lakes area, which can be explored either on foot or by vehicle.

ACKNOWLEDGEMENTS

I would like to thank Dena Stockburger, Sydney Mohr, Brian Leishman, Chris Fisher, Carole Challoner, Gerald Romanchuk, Don Delaney, and Myrna Pearman.

—JOHN ACORN

I would like to thank Dr. Stuart Houston and J. Frank Roy for their mentorship and Nick Saunders for most of the excellent photos in the Saskatchewan section.

—ALAN SMITH

I would like to thank Paula Grieef, Chelsea Enslow, Erin Prokopanko, Michael Bell and Wren Bell, Kristen Martin, Laurel McDonald, Paulson Des Brisay, Lynnea Parker, Laura Burns, Amélie Roberto-Charron, Laurel Moulton, and Katrina Froese of FortWhyte Alive.

A special thanks goes to Rudolf Koes, who wrote the Churchill section, and to the trail-blazing birders of the Manitoba Naturalists Society and Brandon Naturalists Society, who originally identified many of the birding locations described here.

And sincere thanks to Ilya Povalyaev for providing his beautiful photographs to illustrate much of the Manitoba section of the book.

—NICOLA KOPER

ABOUT THE AUTHORS

JOHN ACORN'S birding notes date back to 1976. Born and raised in Edmonton, John has been a lifelong naturalist, interested in everything from insects to birds to fossils. He was the writer and host of two television series, and is the author of some 17 books on natural history subjects. He currently teaches at the University of Alberta, in the Department of Renewable Resources.

ALAN SMITH spent 37 years with the Canadian Wildlife Service, during which time he was involved in the establishment and running of Last Mountain Bird Observatory (LMBO), the only Saskatchewan member of the Canadian Migration Monitoring Network. He is a life member of Nature Saskatchewan, sits on the board of directors of Bird Studies Canada, and is the author of *Atlas of Saskatchewan Birds* and *Saskatchewan Birds*, and the co-author of *Compact Guide to Saskatchewan and Manitoba Birds*.

NICOLA KOPER is a professor of conservation biology at the University of Manitoba, and has studied bird conservation in Canada for most of her academic career. She is also on the board of directors and Scientific Advisory Committees for Nature Conservancy of Canada (Manitoba section). She has co-authored over 50 scientific journal articles in environment and ecology, and has written for popular magazines such as *The Cottager* and *University Affairs*.

INDEX